Praise for *"They're Bankrupting Us!"*

"As someone who has written about the daily lives and struggles of working people, I am constantly impressed and enlightened by Bill Fletcher's work. In *'They're Bankrupting Us!,'* he answers the question of why unions are so essential—not just for economic uplift but for democracy itself. Fletcher is one of our leading labor intellectuals, and once again, he has the last word on a subject of central importance to all Americans."

—Barbara Ehrenreich, author of
Nickel and Dimed: On (Not) Getting By in America

"Coming from a union family helped shape who I am today. Unions have been critical for African Americans, and for all working people, and are essential for social justice. Read Bill Fletcher's important and timely book so we can reassert the humanity of working people and help them stand against the larger societal forces that are trying to crush them."

—Danny Glover, actor/activist

"It's amazing how much nonsense about unions is believed, and how little is really known about their purpose and proud history. Bill Fletcher sets the record straight, and he tells us a thrilling story while doing it. A thriving union movement is crucial to the well-being of working men and women and to the overall health of our democratic way of life. This book—better than any other I've read—explains why."

—Bob Herbert, Distinguished Senior Fellow at Demos
and former New York Times *op-ed columnist*

"Bill Fletcher's new book is a must-read for every worker in America. Full of surprising stories and useful facts, *They're Bankrupting Us!'* uncovers everything we ever wanted to know about how unions work and the true role that unions have played in shaping the nature of our work today."

—*Ai-jen Poo, director, National Domestic Workers Alliance*

"Isn't it curious that the loudest, most venomous voices against unions are the CEOs and Wall Streeters who profit by keeping America's working families down and unions out? In this powerful book, Bill Fletcher exposes their self-serving lies and points out the obvious: unions work. Not only do they advance our economy but also our democracy and our nation's historic pursuit of social justice."

—*Jim Hightower, author, radio commentator,*
public speaker, and editor of the Hightower Lowdown

"Even before I read Bill Fletcher's new book, I knew it was a 'must-read.' Having read it now, my instincts have been confirmed. Bill Fletcher is a brilliant thinker in Ella Baker's tradition. He is an organizer extraordinaire who writes from thirty years' experience in labor and freedom movements. *They're Bankrupting Us!'* speaks to a very broad audience about the diversity, complexity, and vitality of the United States labor movement. And who better to tell that story and teach that lesson than this amazing intellectual, committed activist, and tireless movement teacher?"

—*Barbara Ransby, professor, University of Illinois at Chicago,*
and author of Ella Baker and the Black Freedom Movement

"THEY'RE BANKRUPTING US!"

"THEY'RE BANKRUPTING US!"

And 20 Other Myths about Unions

BILL FLETCHER JR.

BEACON PRESS
BOSTON

BEACON PRESS
25 Beacon Street
Boston, Massachusetts 02108-2892
www.beacon.org

Beacon Press books
are published under the auspices of
the Unitarian Universalist Association of Congregations.

15   14   13   12   8   7   6   5   4   3   2   1

This book is printed on acid-free paper that meets the uncoated paper
ANSI/NISO specifications for permanence as revised in 1992.

Text design and composition by Wilsted & Taylor Publishing Services

Library of Congress Cataloging-in-Publication Data
Fletcher, Bill, Jr.
They're bankrupting us! : and 20 other myths about unions /
Bill Fletcher Jr.
     p. cm.
Includes bibliographical references.
ISBN 978-0-8070-0332-9 (paperback: alk. paper)
1. Labor unions—United States—History. 2. Labor movement—
United States—History. I. Title.
HD6508.F54 2012
331.880973—dc23   2012001302

This book is dedicated to my parents:

JOAN C. FLETCHER AND THE LATE WILLIAM G. FLETCHER SR.

*The fight for social justice will always
be part of the Fletcher household.*

CONTENTS

Introduction · ix
What Is a Union? · xv

Myth 1. "Workers are forced to join unions, right?" · 1
Myth 2. "Unions are bankrupting us and destroying the
　　　　economy." · 8
Myth 3. "Unions are actually run by 'labor bosses,'
　　　　aren't they?" · 20
Myth 4. "Public sector unions cause budget deficits, right?" · 28
Myth 5. "Unions make unreasonable demands that result in lots
　　　　of strikes!" · 38
Myth 6. "Unions were good once, but we don't need them
　　　　any longer." · 48
Myth 7. "Unions are only needed by workers who have problems
　　　　and get into trouble." · 58
Myth 8. "The union uses our money for political action and
　　　　I have no say in the matter!" · 65
Myth 9. "Unions hold me back from advancing, and if I join
　　　　I will never be promoted." · 73
Myth 10. "Unions are corrupt and mobbed up!" · 79
Myth 11. "Unions have a checkered history and were started
　　　　by communists and other troublemakers." · 87
Myth 12. "Unions are all racist and people of color need
　　　　not apply." · 96

Myth 13. "Unions have a history of sexism . . . what makes them
        better now?" · 105

Myth 14. "Unions deal with wages, hours, and working
        conditions; what about other issues?" · 113

Myth 15. "Yes, unions are good for their members, but they hurt
        the rest of us!" · 121

Myth 16. "Unions and corporations are both too big and don't
        really care about the worker." · 129

Myth 17. "Let's face it, in a globalized world, unions
        are powerless." · 134

Myth 18. "Where do unions stand on immigrants—you either
        ignore them or you ignore the rest of us?" · 143

Myth 19. "If unions are so good, why aren't they growing?" · 152

Myth 20. "Unions are so partisan; they always side with the
        Democrats, right?" · 161

Myth 21. "If unions are so great, why aren't more people around
        the world forming them?" · 169

Concluding Thoughts · 178
Acknowledgments · 186
Notes · 188

INTRODUCTION

There comes a time in any war where one side or the other makes a gamble that the moment has arrived for what is known as "the final offensive." In some cases, there has been a long stalemate, while in others one side simply feels that it is strategically positioned to finish off their adversary. In a final offensive, there is an all-out mobilization aimed at eliminating the opponent or of so crippling them that they have no alternative but to surrender.

There has been an ongoing war against working people and unions both within the United States and globally. This "war" revolves around power and the distribution of wealth. From the moment unions emerged in the United States in the early nineteenth century, the forces of wealth and business have largely been arrayed against unionization efforts, seeing in them mechanisms that could potentially weaken their power over workers. In fact, the history of labor/business relations in the United States has been the bloodiest of any advanced industrial country, mostly because of the extent to which efforts at worker self-organization have been repressed by the forces of business, often through brute force.

In the post–World War II era, organized labor believed it had achieved a modus vivendi, an agreement to disagree, with major sections of the business community, primarily in the North, Midwest, and on the West Coast. Yet, for a variety of reasons that we will explore, organized labor ceased to grow and instead entered what was initially a slow and then a steady decline. After 1980, that slow but steady decline accelerated into a drop of catastrophic proportions. Despite this, many leaders of organized labor refused to accept the ramifications of the situation and adjust course. Largely this is what is meant when someone speaks of a crisis of organized labor today.

The "final offensive" against organized labor was fully launched in the aftermath of Wisconsin governor Scott Walker's proposed cut of collective bargaining rights and the subsequent nationwide protests in March 2011. It's important to appreciate that this attack, underway for decades, began anew when Ronald Reagan was elected president in 1980. Prior to Reagan's victory, there were individuals and factions within the Republican Party that accepted at least some elements of the New Deal reforms of the 1930s, and generally, if grudgingly, accepted the existence of labor unions. What changed with Reagan was the Republican philosophy on the economy and, with that, the approach to be taken toward labor unions.

What Reagan, Reaganism, and what came to ultimately be known as "neoliberalism" represented was a complete rejection of the role of government as an instrument for the fair distribution of wealth in order to address the unfortunate, the unemployed, the underemployed, and the disregarded. Also contained in the logic of this philosophy was both the notion that anything that represented an obstacle to the accumulation of profits should be removed, and that individuals shouldn't concern themselves with the collective good, and should only think about "number 1." In the early stages of neoliberalism, the focus was on government-controlled industries, government functions that the private sector sought, and government regulations that the private sector wished to eliminate. In time, obstacles to the accumulation of profits more clearly came to include organizations of workers and farmers—that is, organizations that sought to equalize wealth and bring about economic justice, if not social justice. Organized labor constituted a major obstacle to their agenda as far as the proponents of neoliberalism were concerned.

Despite the fact that US unions never represented more than 35 percent of the nonagricultural workforce—a considerable percentage by today's standards—unions were nevertheless a part of the so-called mainstream. Therefore, to move against unions there needed to be—again utilizing a military analogy—a softening-up operation. In other words, a direct attack on the very existence of unions would not be efficacious, at least initially, so the proponents of neoliberalism began to ideologically challenge the relevance and appropriateness of labor unions by sowing confusion and misinformation among the general public. This was accompanied by an increased hostility by employers at both the bargaining table and in places where workers chose to join or form labor unions (including but not limited to the National Labor Relations Board union certification elections).

Many will be surprised to hear that the first salvo was actually fired under President Jimmy Carter when, in 1978, he terminated nearly two hundred postal workers who had been engaged in a wildcat strike. This was a significant step but received very little national attention. What did receive attention three years later was when President Reagan turned on his erstwhile allies in PATCO (Professional Air Traffic Controllers Organization) and terminated them en masse for the strike they undertook. This firing, ironically taken by a former president of the Screen Actors Guild, sent shockwaves throughout both labor and business communities. It was followed by myriad concession demands on unions by employers across various industries and was characterized by plant closings and brazen violations of the National Labor Relations Act by employers who were determined to avoid, at virtually all costs, dealing equitably with a labor union chosen by the workers.

It was with the PATCO firings that an all-out assault on organized labor began. To conduct these assaults, various myths were unleashed by the propagandists for the wealthy and big business. Some of these myths are quite old; others new; and still others are warmed-over versions of assertions made since the rise of labor unionism. In still other cases, legitimate criticisms of unions were elevated to categorical attacks to serve undemocratic and anti-worker objectives.

This book dispels these myths, categorical attacks, and broad-brush criticisms and clarifies why labor unions are essential for democracy. To be clear, I believe that unions are indispensable for democracy, but also they are far from a panacea. As you will see, there are accurate and appropriate criticisms that must be made of labor unions and the practice of labor unionism, yet such criticisms are not aimed to tear down but rather promote something that would be akin to a "labor reformation," to borrow a term from my friend, mentor and long-time labor activist Jerry Tucker.

One of the great ironies of history is that the United States has had a long and significant experience with unions, an experience that the rest of the world knows more about than most Americans. The first labor political parties, for example, were formed during the early to mid-nineteenth century, sometimes on a citywide basis with later efforts at nationwide parties. May Day, as International Workers' Day, came about because of the struggle for the eight-hour day on US soil. International Women's Day also originated in the United States out of the struggle of women workers in the first decade of the twentieth century. Consider also that Dr. Martin Luther King Jr., who had a long and distinguished history of being committed to workers' struggles, was killed while supporting striking sanitation workers. The Ku Klux Klan, a nefarious organization by any standards, was not only an organization opposed to blacks, Jews, Catholics, Latinos, and Asians, but also one that some employers utilized against workers trying to organize labor unions. We should also consider migrants in the United States, specifically, African Americans, Chicanos, and Puerto Ricans. They moved across the country in search of a better life and encountered many of the same problems that today's immigrants have faced: low-wage employment with few protections, racial/ethnic animosity, and ambiguity from the official union movement as to whether they even had a place in organized labor. Moreover, consider one more fact: did you know that in the late 1920s, mainstream publications and academics were predicting the final and complete demise of unions and their replacement with either employer-controlled organizations or an everyone-against-everyone workplace existence? Few of us know this history, and the absence of such historical knowledge makes us vulnerable to demagogues.

This book is not only a refutation of attacks and misinformation—it is also personal. I grew up in a profoundly pro-union family at a time when certain things were understood, such as, you do not cross picket lines; it is the right thing for workers to have unions and bargain collectively; and, it is good for *all* workers to have a pension and health care. My family always made it clear that unions are needed because there is a fundamental power imbalance in this society between those with money, who control business and finance, and the rest of us.

Yet, interestingly, my parents were never Pollyannaish about unions and, in fact, one of my earliest memories concerning unions was an observation my father made. He said, "Bill, there are two sorts of unions in this country. There are those that are mobbed up and racist. And then there are those like the union led by Harry Bridges.[1] That latter represents real unionism."

For years I didn't fully grasp what my father meant, but I eventually came to understand that unions and unionism aren't monolithic. You can stand for a certain principle or practice, but someone else using the same words can represent something markedly different. Inspired by my parents, other relatives, my sister, my close social justice activist associates, and a former college professor of mine (the late Dr. Ewart Guinier, father of Professor Lani Guinier), I embarked on a journey to enter into and, I hoped, contribute toward influencing the labor union movement in a positive direction. My quest has taken me from working several years as a welder in a shipyard, to community organizing, to serving as a staff person in four unions, to a senior staff position in the AFL-CIO, the main federation of labor unions in the United States. I have interacted with trade unionists from foreign labor movements, as well as reformers and insurgents in the US trade union movement, all working to construct an energized twenty-first-century labor movement.

This book not only flows from the knowledge I have gained over the years, but from the heart. All genuine trade unionists feel attached to a lineage that harkens back hundreds of years. We feel linked to the early bond servants (indentured servants) who rebelled against those who held them in near captivity for at least seven years. We are connected to the slaves who were held in actual captivity, defined by their black skins as supposedly inferior to both rob them of their wealth as well as mislead the non-slave (so-called white) as to what was really happening. We feel a bond to the Chicano and Native American miners and mill workers in the Southwest, as well as Asian workers who built the railroads and tilled so many fields. And we feel a link to the European immigrants who lived and worked in stifling conditions around environmentally toxic workplaces. We feel the linkage with those workers who have resisted injustice and insisted upon receiving justice and dignity, sometimes at the cost of their own lives.

Let me conclude with a famous story that originates with the ancient African fabulist Aesop (often incorrectly identified as Greek). It takes place in a mythical era when humans and lions could speak to and understand one another. A man and a lion encountered each other in the jungle, and they decided to walk together, soon finding themselves embroiled in an argument over who was superior. Suddenly they came across a clearing where there was a statue of Hercules standing astride a lion. The man pointed at the statue, asserting this was proof that humans were superior to lions. The lion astutely replied that had lions built the statue, no doubt the lion would tower over Hercules.

Too often history is "top-down" and told from the perspective of those who build the statues, and indeed the history of labor and working people has often been written by outsiders. Given the numerous myths and damaging misperceptions about unions today, I am responding to the call to correct the errors, misinformation, and caricature so we can build our own beautiful and enduring statues and, in so doing, set the record straight.

WHAT IS A UNION?

It is declared to be the policy of the United States to eliminate
the causes of certain substantial obstructions to the free flow
of commerce and to mitigate and eliminate these obstructions
when they have occurred by encouraging the practice and procedure of collective bargaining and by protecting the exercise
by workers of full freedom of association, self-organization,
and designation of representatives of their own choosing, for
the purpose of negotiating the terms and conditions of their
employment or other mutual aid or protection.
                                   —*from the National Labor Relations Act*

In early 2011, as I was flying from San Jose, California, to San Diego,
I was engrossed reading *Global Restructuring, Labour and the Challenges for Transnational Solidarity*. The woman sitting next to me was
noticeably interested in my book, so we struck up a conversation.
She was in her thirties and lived with her husband and two children in northern California. When she inevitably asked what I was
reading, I explained it was about the global labor movement and the
challenges of globalization. She looked at me intently while I explained, and when I finished she asked, "What's a union?"

To say that I was startled by her question would be a serious un-
derstatement. But this woman was sincere, so I went on to explain
what a union was and gave her a couple of examples, such as teach-
ers' unions. She nodded her head, and that might have ended the
matter, but I suddenly realized that in spite of my explanation, she
still didn't entirely understand. It seemed I was explaining something with which she was, apparently, entirely unfamiliar. What

made this both perplexing yet instructive is that this was obviously an intelligent individual, and I fear her ignorance is emblematic of many Americans who don't fundamentally understand the raison d'être behind the labor movement.

A friend of mine, noted labor strategist and organizer Bob Muehlenkamp, has a simple answer: it's an organization of workers. At one level, it's that uncomplicated—an organization of workers created for a specific set of objectives.

At the same time, this definition is only an icebreaker. There are various sorts of worker organizations, ranging from sports clubs to industrial cooperatives. There are, however, a few distinguishing characteristics of a labor union:

1. It's an organization based upon collective self-interest that focuses on issues relative to work, specifically, and to the economy, more generally. As such, it seeks to bargain on behalf of a group of workers to improve their living and working conditions.
2. It can be organized based on a specific workplace, a type of work, an industry, or in some cases, a specific geography, and seeks to build an identity of interests for these workers.
3. It attempts to take wages out of competition between workers who are fighting to improve their respective living standards, thereby opposing favoritism.
4. It seeks fairness for workers, and specifically, fair treatment by employers and governments. At their best, unions seek to democratize the workplace.

These are general characteristics, but each of them raises crucial questions. For our purposes, let's just mention two: (1) Who are the "workers"? and (2) What is meant by "fairness"?

There's no hard and fast response because the answers depend on your vision for what needs to be done and who you believe has a common interest. Confused yet? Perhaps a little background will help flesh out the picture.

WHERE DID LABOR UNIONS COME FROM?

In any workplace, there's a power imbalance between those who work and those who hire workers, own the machinery, and give the orders. Workers, through their labor power, produce things to be sold. But these things (whether manufactured, services, or intellectual property) can't be sold at cost (which includes the workers' wages, heating/cooling, and raw materials) because the owner wouldn't profit. Instead, they're sold at a price that depends on both the amount of time, energy, and expertise put into the product, along with what the market will accept. The owner then takes a profit; some of it is reinvested into the business and some of that goes to the owner.

In a modern, democratic capitalist society, a worker can choose to leave their employment when they wish. However, the employer may also get rid of the worker. They may do this for economic reasons, for instance, a layoff due to a decline in business, or they may terminate the worker because they simply wish to get rid of them. In fact, termination or firing is often referred to as the "capital punishment" of employment law. Although an employer may suffer a temporary problem, such as work flow when a worker leaves voluntarily, a worker can suffer more dramatically by not being able to afford food and shelter. It's vital to note this because there's no equivalency between the employee's ability to leave versus the employer's ability to fire. Simply put, the consequences are considerably different. Added to this, there is no due process when there is a termination, unless the termination is specifically unlawful.

Most of us who have to work to survive recognize we're in a constant state of competition with other workers. Let's say you go looking for work. An employer may hire you based on criteria such as age, skills, race, gender, ethnicity, or what you are willing to accept as your wage or salary. Let's focus on this last matter, for a moment.

There's an exercise to use to see how competition works among workers, that is, how they have to compete and how that competition can be used against them by those with power. Think about a good salary and benefit package for a specific job. Now, ask the people in your group to, by a show of hands, indicate who would be willing to work at that rate. Probably most hands will go up. Then reduce the salary, wage, or benefit package by a little. Ask for another show of hands to see who would work for this amount. Keep lowering the rate. Here's what you will most likely find:

1. As you lower the salary, wage, or benefit package, hands will stay up, but the number of hands will decrease.
2. There will be points where you yourself would probably not accept going any lower but someone else will.
3. There will come a time when no one will raise their hand, i.e., you have reached the point that the group has decided that it simply cannot accept such deterioration in their living standards.

What you have just seen is one important way that capitalism drives workers to compete with one another. There are frequently some workers who, because of their circumstances, are willing or compelled to accept a lower salary, wage, or benefit package than others. This is not a moral statement—it speaks to their desperation or life circumstances. Younger workers, for instance, tend to think less about pensions and retirement, whereas those are more pressing concerns for middle-aged and older workers.

Later I'll discuss some of the other divisions that exist or emerge among workers, but let's start with a basic point: because of different life circumstances, workers can effectively be pitted against one another by employers. Therefore, to decrease the likelihood that workers will be played against one another—that is, are victims of favoritism—the workers have to take measures to decrease the competition among them. One such measure is creating a labor union.

Throughout history, there has always been some form of worker organization, but with the rise of capitalism, there emerged certain organizations that aimed to decrease competition between workers. Known as "guilds," these organizations evolved out of the Middle Ages in Europe and some parts of Africa and Asia as a means to control a specific skill. These guilds regulated how laborers were trained and, through apprenticeships, limited the number of laborers in any given craft, ensuring that those who worked would have a relatively stable income (at least in theory).

Employers responded to these guilds and other similar organizations by changing the way that work was done. Employers sought to reduce their dependency on a specific guild (or other such organization) and to weaken the control that those workers had over the production process. An example of this was the introduction of new technology for the production of clothing, making it possible to produce items faster but also with less reliance on a small number of skilled workers.

In addition to guilds, insurrectionary organizations challenged the economic system as a whole, rather than simply negotiating for control over work or better conditions. Examples of these include bond servant/indentured servant revolts in the 1600s that challenged indentured servitude, and also slave conspiracies and insurrections that challenged slavery. These insurrectionary organizations took various forms, but they and early labor unions often resembled one another and were often treated similarly by the powers that be: violent repression. In both cases, insurrectionary organizations and the early labor movement had to begin covertly. There were no laws protecting the early labor movement, and there were certainly no laws protecting indentured servants and slaves that revolted. Both of these forms of organization resembled secret societies, sometimes down to specific rituals that were practiced when new members joined. It, therefore, should not be a surprise as to the level of anti-worker violence that has been carried out throughout the colonial and postcolonial history of what came to be known as the United States of America.

In sum, unions are formed by workers to press for an improvement in their living standards and to reduce the competition among them, a competition that isn't the result of some intrinsic desire to compete but is due to the nature of capitalism, which pits worker against worker to improve the employer's bottom line. Unions emerge within capitalism because of a fundamental power imbalance between workers and employers. While they seek an improvement in the living standards for those they represent, they may or may not have a clear vision as to what that ultimately means besides wages/salaries, benefits, and working conditions. In this sense, they are quite different from political parties.

SO, WHAT ABOUT THE QUESTIONS?

Labor unions are not defined by any blueprint. In the United States, unions are protected and legally recognized by the National Labor Relations Act (NLRA), otherwise known as the Wagner Act, which was signed into law by President Franklin Roosevelt in 1935. The NLRA gave national legitimacy to unions. The creation and passage of this act came about by a combination of factors, including the turbulence of the Great Depression, the rise of socialist movements (and countries) as an alternative to capitalism, Roosevelt's need for allies against the so-called "economic royalists" (for instance, the right-wing business interests that would make no compromises with working people), and the rise of a workers' movement from among the unemployed as well as from the mass production industries (such as, steel, auto, rubber, bread, cigarettes), which had been largely unorganized until then.[1] The authors of the NLRA were especially concerned that worker militancy be brought under control and that "industrial peace," as they defined it at the time, be established. This necessitated the establishment of a system that, at least in some respects, spoke to the demands of workers for the right of self-organization and collective bargaining.

The NLRA created a National Labor Relations Board (NLRB), a form of a labor court system, to resolve disputes between unions and employers, particularly those disputes that arise when workers are joining or forming labor unions. For example, let's say workers in a hospital choose to organize a union. Hospital management may argue that the nurses shouldn't be in the same union as so-called nonprofessional workers (technical or janitorial). If this goes to the NLRB, they'll decide who's eligible to join the union. If it doesn't go to the NLRB, then the workers will reach a decision through negotiations with the employer. In other cases, workers organize according to a specific skill or craft. For instance, in the construction and building trades, it's normal to have unions that represent a specific set of workers, such as, a union for carpenters or for painters.[2]

The fact that workers are organized according to specific craft, skill, or workplace guidelines can create a particular "them versus us" mentality that pits workers in one trade against another, or workers in one industry against another, or even workers in the *same* industry against one another. There are countless examples of this. Feuds that take place, for instance, in the building trades/construction industry between unions representing different crafts. Or the sense in some unions for manufacturing workers that their issues are not valued by public sector or service worker unions is yet another example. Keep in mind that unions are different from most organizations because they are not formed based on any specific ideology. Rather, they are more like a *coalition* of workers and, therefore, have certain common interests as well as very different ones. Sometimes this unity brings them together but has them look out for their own interests in narrow ways. As a result, unions aren't monoliths and can vary on different social issues, how they operate, who they seek to organize and represent, etc.

The punch line, as it were, is that what unions actually do and can accomplish largely depends on the workers themselves and the leadership they elect. There are, of course, external factors that help influence a union's success, but being aware of history illuminates how and why a particular union operates as it does. The remainder of this book will help the reader better understand how some unions can be outstanding champions of social and economic justice, while other unions can be narrow, cliquish, and in some cases, outright corrupt.

"WORKERS ARE FORCED TO JOIN UNIONS, RIGHT?"

One of the charges often thrown at unions is that they are somehow undemocratic because workers must join them if they work in a unionized workplace. Using words and terms that sound democratic or libertarian, voices are raised that suggest that workers are being whipped into an organization they want nothing to do with. The reality is very different.

Labor unions are created and recognized by an employer when the *majority* of workers in a particular company decide they want to form or join a union. This may happen through an election or another process in which workers indicate they want to be part of this labor union, which an employer then recognizes.

What happens after a labor union is formed/certified/recognized at a specific company or within a specific industry depends on the power of the workers *and* the law, but it is shaped, at least from the standpoint of the unionized workers, by a very specific problem: maintaining and shoring up their security as a group of organized workers.

Let's think about the situation facing workers by analogizing it to what has been called the "prisoner's dilemma." The gist of this scenario is that two prisoners are locked in separate cells and are each offered a deal. If they stand firm and keep to the same story, they will be released or receive a minimum sentence of a month.

But the jailers are trying to get the prisoners to sell each other out. Whoever talks first gets the better deal; but not only that, if one talks and the other remains silent, the one who remains silent is incarcerated for one year while the one who talks is released. If they both turn on each other, they are both sentenced to three months.

In the world of work, workers are constantly exposed to the prisoner's dilemma. The employer in a non-union setting plays his/her favorites and pits one set of workers against the other. Once a union is formed, the employer does not normally give up on this. The employer hopes to minimize the strength of the union by discouraging workers from joining, often promising or suggesting they will get a better deal if they do not. The employer may even hold up an example of someone who chose not to join the union and instead became a supervisor or received some other "gift."

The dilemma for the workers who have formed the union is, therefore, clear. If they do nothing, the employer may be able to convince enough workers not to join the union, thereby dividing the workforce and diminishing resources. As a result, the workers lack any power to push for their concerns. Rather than the union being able to represent all the workers, as mandated by the NLRA, the employer can create a situation where some workers convince themselves that they may get the better deal by staying outside of the union.

As a result of this dilemma, most unions push for what is called "union security agreements." Depending on the law of a particular state—which may or may not allow any of this—a union can win an agreement with the employer that as a condition of employment and after a specific time, workers who are legally represented by a union must become members of that union. This does not mean that they must be active in the union, but rather, in accordance with the law, the labor union in a specific workplace is the *exclusive representative* of all the workers, and they must join the union. There cannot be two unions representing the same set of workers, and neither can a specific set of workers decide to obtain an independent representative (like an attorney) to represent their interests vis-à-vis the employer. The union must represent all workers that it's legally entitled to represent in a nondiscriminatory fashion. This is called a "union shop" agreement. Where someone has legitimate religious objections to being part of a union, they are generally exempted from participation. The main point, however, is that a "union shop" is not something imposed on the workers but is the result of the workers themselves who created the union in the first place. This desire of the majority not to allow management to play workers off against one another has driven the demand for union shops.

In some cases where a union is unable to win a union shop agreement or where the law prevents that, the union may win what is called an "agency agreement" or "fee payer agreement." This means that workers do not have to join the union, but they pay a fee, essentially the cost of representation, as a condition of employment. An apt analogy is auto insurance. You may be an excellent driver, but if there's an accident, you need to be covered. Agency agreements provide for protection—"insurance"—for workers even if they choose not to join, but with the workers providing a fee to help defray the costs.

Now, here's where things get complicated. In 1947, Congress authorized states to implement what are called "Right to Work" statutes. The term is a misnomer because there is no right to *work* guaranteed by such statutes. These statutes exist in the South and Southwest, as well as in several other states. They are being actively pushed more broadly in the United States by business groups as a way of weakening the power of workers. Let's look at how they operate and why I call them a misnomer.

Right to Work laws prohibit union security agreements. They basically state that a worker does not need to join the union or pay any sort of fee; however, the union *must* represent that worker at its (the union's) own expense. The actual point of a Right to Work law, then, is to drain the union of resources and simultaneously appeal to selfishness on the part of individual workers. The phrasings of right to work statutes suggest they are about freedom of choice. Actually, they are not. They're about weakening the ability of workers—as a group—from exerting any sort of power.

To return to the auto insurance analogy, states pass laws that mandate that, in order to own and drive a car, you must have auto insurance. If you have a license and go to a car rental agency without insurance, you'll need to purchase it from the company. If you refuse to purchase it, you are liable for the car. As a driver, you can't say that if you have an accident and have chosen not to obtain insurance that it's up to the government or anyone else to cover your costs. You are stuck. You are liable. But it gets worse. As anyone who has had an accident with an unlicensed or uninsured driver knows, there may be no way to collect anything from him or her. They may be so broke that the entire weight of the accident falls on the victim rather than the person responsible. A worker who refuses to contribute to the cost of representation is the equivalent of an uninsured driver. He is taking a chance not only with his own safety but also with that of his coworkers.

An individual worker may decide he doesn't want to pay union dues. He may make the argument—which we will discuss later—that he will not have a problem at work, so why should he have to pay? Except, what happens if, for some reason, he is treated unfairly and wishes to contest such treatment? Who should have to pay for his right to fairness?

If you think of unions as a sort of society at work, then that society is mandated to look out for the whole. It, therefore, needs the participation of everyone who is affected by the conditions of work to be involved. The failure to have union security agreements is a very real problem for unions and workers. In the federal system, there are no union shop agreements or agency fee agreements. You can, therefore, have a situation such as the one faced by the American Federation of Government Employees (the largest of the unions in the federal sector) where it has, as of mid-2011, approximately 260,000 members *but represents more than 600,000 workers.*

Let's think about this for a moment: 260,000 individual workers, who have voluntarily agreed to join the union, are being asked to pay for the representation costs of themselves plus an additional 340,000 workers. What are those representation costs? Here are a few examples:

1. First, if a worker chooses to file a grievance because of an alleged injustice, the grievances need to be investigated and may go to what is known as "binding arbitration" where an independent individual—the equivalent of a judge—decides the merits of the case. The judge, actually known as an arbitrator, is compensated.
2. A second involves salary. In the federal system, the unions are forbidden from negotiating wages and salaries set by Congress. This means that for wages, salaries, and benefits to improve—or to ensure they are not stripped away— pressure and advocacy must be brought to the halls of Congress. When a union goes to Congress, it's not advocating for its members alone, but for all it legally represents. Doing the research, preparing the arguments, doing any media work, and all other such activities cost money. This is part of ensuring representation.
3. Health and safety is another area. While any individual worker has the right to contact the Occupational Health and Safety Administration (OSHA), the union has individuals who are trained to identify health and safety dangers and to negotiate with management regarding these.

Each of these three areas can be, and often are, taken for granted by individual workers. Many choose not to join the union, and therefore not contribute toward representation, because they believe they will get this representation in either case. But think for a moment about the prisoner's dilemma. Any one individual may be able to withhold his contribution toward representation and that will more than likely have no overall impact. But when a critical mass of workers chooses not to contribute, yet expects they will be taken care of, there is always the risk that the overall organization will suffer a crisis and be unable to deliver on any of its promises. To put it another way, successful representation depends on the participation of the workers, at the very least through financial contributions, but also ideally by volunteering time to build the organization.

Here's a true story told to me by a good friend that illustrates the problem: "I used to play tennis with a guy who worked in the post office. He also had a part-time job as a chaplain at the local hospital. He had told me that he was against joining the union, mainly because he was a good worker and would never need one. Unions were only for bad workers, he explained. Sometime later, management had changed his schedule unilaterally and reduced his total work hours. Not only was he making less, but the work also interfered with his chaplaincy job—the one that was more important to him. I saw him several days later. He told me he called the union and that they went to management right away and got his regular work schedule reinstated. I asked him if he thought better about unions, if he would join as a result of their assistance, and if he realizes that union dues made it possible for him to get help for being unfairly treated. He said he still refused to join the union. I pointed out to him that for a chaplain who talked about goodness, he was 'freeloading'—my exact word. He wanted something for nothing."

So, are workers "forced" to join unions? The bottom line is that whether one must become a member of a union is determined by the agreement negotiated between the workers (through their union) and the employer (and any applicable law). But the real bottom line is that when an institution is mandated to exclusively represent all members of a specific group there is a cost involved. There is no "free lunch," as they say. That institution has an interest in the participation of all it must represent; otherwise, it cannot function. For this reason, the so-called libertarian arguments do not hold water. One cannot pay the social costs only when one needs the assistance. This is the objection, in the larger society, to

those who argue that they should not have to pay for public education if they do not use it. To guarantee the *scale* of assistance, there
must be involvement by all who are affected, and all who may *potentially* use or need the assistance. This is all that unions ask, and
nothing more.

MYTH 2

"UNIONS ARE BANKRUPTING US AND DESTROYING THE ECONOMY."

Even in the face of efforts to bring down the soaring US budget deficit, military spending continues to receive privileged treatment. President Obama's FY2012 budget announced a five-year freeze on non-security-related discretionary expenditure, but military spending, along with other security spending such as intelligence and Homeland Security is exempt. . . . Taken together, these figures suggest that the United States continues to prioritize maintaining its overwhelming military power as the basis of its security and status.[1]

In discussions about the economy, deficits, bankruptcy, and so forth, it's useful to ask some pointed questions interrogating the assumptions we often make. For this reason, I begin this discussion with a quote concerning US military expenditures rather than something having to do with organized labor.

Let's consider, for a moment, what this study reveals. Despite the urgent call for government to address the alleged dangers of budget deficits, until very recently military expenditures continued to climb. In fact, there has been an unspoken bipartisan understanding that the military is to be treated very carefully when it comes to consideration of cuts. Despite claims to the contrary, the disastrous impact of military expenditures on the deficit has been ignored, at least until the summer 2011's so-called deficit crisis (and the beginning of discussions regarding cutting back on military expenditures). And any possible correlation between such expenditures and the United States's economic plight is largely disregarded in mainstream or elite opinion.

One can also consider the issue of health-care costs. In the absence of a true national health insurance—Medicare for All or a similar approach—health-care costs continue to rise and become a greater tug on the overall economy.[2] The cost for single individuals in 2011 is an average of $5,429 (8 percent more than in 2010) and for families $15,073 (9 percent over 2010). And with such rising costs, along with increased unemployment, the numbers of uninsured continue to rise, meaning that any medical care they receive must be done on an emergency-room basis at the exorbitant rates associated with such care. Those costs fall on the government, that is, on the taxpayer.

Compare both of these examples to the attitude of the mainstream establishment toward labor unions and their role in the economy. The suggestion that labor unions are the source of economic problems that have increasingly plagued the United States isn't based on fact, but rather, derives from an ideological narrative.

Contrary to how we may have learned it in school, history is not simply a collection of facts. It is the assemblage of facts within a framework that prioritizes certain information. For example, the history of slavery can be told from the viewpoint of the slave owner—or that of the slave, yielding vastly different narratives.

So, too, is it with the economy. To borrow from the words of the late Harvard economist John Kenneth Galbraith, mainstream economists do not like to call capitalism "capitalism" because doing so calls attention to who or what is the dominant factor in our societies—capital! For this reason, terms such as "free market economy"[3] are used to obscure the power relations of our society and mask how the economy actually works.

Because the members of the economic elite have largely opposed labor unions since they first arose in the 1830s, they've sought to justify repressing unions while convincing the larger public of their alleged harm. As such, they've created a story that goes something like this:

> The United States was founded on hard work by individuals
> without the assistance of government. Through hard work
> and free enterprise, tremendous advances were made. If you
> had a great idea, you could become rich—you just needed to
> be persistent. If your ideas made no sense, then the free mar-
> ket would settle accounts. But labor unions have interfered
> in this process by discouraging individuals from taking risks
> and protecting those who shouldn't be protected.

This ideological narrative ignores significant facts, portraying labor unions as a force that has derailed the natural order of things. As Galbraith noted, this story ignores the power relations that exist in society and assumes everyone is on an even playing field.

To use the example of US military expenditures, it is important to keep in mind that they dwarf those of any other country. In 2010, world military expenditures were approximately $1.62 trillion with US expenditures representing 43 percent of this total.[4] Explanations about why our expenditures need to be so high often turn to gibberish. The United States is followed in expenditures by countries such as China and Russia, but they aren't even remotely in the same ballpark, despite the periodic references to the alleged military threat that the Chinese currently present. In fact, our military expenditures amount to the combined expenditures of the next fifteen countries in order after the United States! So, in a period of economic and financial scarcity, we are told that roughly $700 billion should be ignored due to threats to national security. This is not a matter of rational economic calculations, but ideological assumptions.

If we are to further examine the macro level, we will see other areas of concern regarding the economy that should be an equal worry to the impact of military expenditures. Although at times mentioned in the mainstream media, wealth disparity rarely gets the political or economic attention it deserves (at least until the rise of the Occupy Wall Street movement), yet historically, wealth polarization has been a highly destabilizing force.

To understand wealth polarization, consider the following report by the Center on Budget and Policy Priorities.

> Put together by the Center on Budget and Policy Priorities. . . .
> It shows that the 30 years following the Second World War
> were a time of broadly shared prosperity: Income for the
> bottom 90 percent of American households roughly kept
> pace with economic growth.
>
> But over the last 35 years, there's been an abrupt shift:
> Total growth has slowed marginally, but the real change has
> been in how the results of that growth are distributed. Now,
> the bottom 90 percent have seen their income rise only by a
> tiny fraction of total growth, while income for the richest 1
> percent has exploded by upwards of 275 percent.[5]

Actually, the situation is even more troubling than these figures suggest. The conditions of working people have steadily declined since the mid-1970s, bringing the workers' living standard to roughly what it was in the mid-1960s once inflation is factored. Given this phenomenon, it's easier to understand the personal debt crisis. Working people, and much of the bottom 70 to 90 percent of the population, have sought to sustain a decent living standard and have only been able to do this by going deeper into personal debt.

The Washington, DC–based think tank Economic Policy Institute (EPI), in looking at the question of wealth in light of the 2007–2009 recession (which, for working people, has lasted far longer), described the impact of the economic decline in stark terms. In line with the analysis cited above, the top of the rich, the *Forbes 400*, saw its average wealth increase by 633 percent from 1982 to 2000: from $509 million to $3.7 billion. In 2009, this same group averaged $3.2 billion in wealth, up 523 percent from 1982. Contrast this with the rest of the population. In 2009, nearly one in four households had zero or negative net worth, while 37.1 percent had net worth of less than $12,000. This situation has been particularly acute in communities of color.[6] Ironically, this report also debunked one of the major myths about wealth possession in the United States: i.e., stock holdings. The report noted that even in 2007, prior to the recession, half all US households owned *no* stocks at all, either directly or indirectly through mutual funds or retirement funds.[7]

One will notice that this vast economic inequality which so damages the socioeconomic framework has nothing to do with unions but rather is centered on the elite, specifically, the top 5 to 10 percent of the population. This wealth polarization was not the consequence of some natural evolution but instead resulted from policies that advanced the interests of the elite.

Beginning in 1964, corporate tax rates began to decrease, dropping from 52 percent to 48 percent over two years. The Revenue Act of 1978, which introduced changes to capital gains taxes to stimulate the economy, caused the top rate of long-term gains to drop from 50 percent to 28 percent.[8]

Corporations and wealthy taxpayers, the holders of capital, were the immediate beneficiaries of these cuts. With the 1981 Economic Recovery Tax Act (ERTA), President Reagan initiated drops to the entire rate structure of the tax system by 25 percent over three years. The act also produced significant decreases in estate and gift taxes.[9]

The Tax Reform Act of 1986, touted by his supporters as Reagan's greatest achievement, supposedly "brought the average marginal tax rates on labor and capital income closer together."[10] This was supposed to be achieved by broadening the tax base. Tax brackets were consolidated from fifteen to four, and income rates of the poorest taxpayers increased from 11 percent to 15 percent. Meanwhile, the income tax rate of the wealthiest individuals was reduced from 50 percent to 28 percent.[11] The act also eliminated tax deductions on IRA contributions by high-income taxpayers.[12]

Federal deficits wrought by these tax cuts later compelled

President George H. W. Bush to increase the income tax rate on the wealthiest bracket from 28 percent to 31 percent, despite his famous promise of no new taxes.

More recently, the George W. Bush tax cuts of 2001 and 2003 lowered rates for families that earned double the median income, and left rates for median income families unchanged. The benefits of these cuts are clear: if made permanent, the Bush tax cuts are projected to funnel 31 percent of the cuts' benefits to only the top 1 percent of the wealthiest taxpayers.[13]

The corporate income tax rate in the United States, currently at 35 percent, is the second highest in the world. Loopholes, tax shelters, and subsidies, though, contribute to a general climate of corporate tax avoidance that is rampant in the economy.[14]

This last point about tax loopholes cannot be overstated. To give an example, *Dollars & Sense* notes General Electric has benefited immensely from such loopholes: "General Electric, the third largest U.S. corporation, turned a profit of $10.3 billion in 2010, paid no corporate income taxes, and got a 'tax benefit' of $1.1 billion on taxes owed on past profits. And from 2005 to 2009, according to GE's filings, the corporation paid a consolidated tax rate of just 11.6 percent on its corporate rates, including state, local, and foreign taxes. That's a far cry from the 35 percent rate nominally levied on corporate profits above $10 million."[15]

To a great extent, the conditions of the wealthy and taxes are analogous to the distinction between form and reality: while the tax rate for corporations may appear high, what corporations actually pay is a different matter.[16]

But there is another side to this discussion. The wrecking of the economy and the destruction of the living standard held by millions (through about 1980) is tied to changes that have taken place in global capitalism. We will be discussing this matter—*corporate or neoliberal globalization*—a bit later. For now, it's important to note that while the capitalist economic system has always been global (remember the slave trade), the economy has become profoundly more interconnected in the last thirty years through trade deals, political/policy changes orchestrated by governments, and the introduction of new technologies. Little of this has been to the benefit of working people.

In the early 1990s, the public was sold the idea that one major trade deal, the North American Free Trade Agreement (NAFTA), which linked the United States, Mexico, and Canada, would result in tremendous benefits. Though there was large-scale opposition to this trade deal, it was passed by Congress and signed into law by President Bill Clinton. In NAFTA's first decade, the United States developed large trade deficits with Canada—particularly in manufacturing—that by 2004 had displaced hundreds of thousands of US jobs, many of them unionized jobs.[17] With regard to Mexico, by 2010, NAFTA had resulted in a $97.2 billion US trade deficit that displaced 682,900 jobs.

It's important to understand that, contrary to Ross Perot's notion that NAFTA represented a "giant sucking sound" of jobs going to Mexico, the situation was actually far more complex. Working people in *all three NAFTA countries* suffered because of the trade deal. In fact, employment in Mexico has become very precarious, and the agricultural system is in disarray. Contrary to public wisdom, Mexico lost 1.3 million jobs in its agricultural sector due to cheap, subsidized corn from the United States.[18] This fact alone helps one understand the steady rise in migration since 1994.

From the standpoint of the economic elite, who have benefitted from such treaties, free trade agreements such as NAFTA have been a stunning success. At the same time, and from the standpoint of working people in these countries, NAFTA hasn't been lucrative. Jobs have been lost, towns destroyed, and hundreds of thousands of people have been forced to migrate internally or by crossing borders (legally or otherwise).

This snapshot at the transnational level suggests that the problems with the US economy have little to do with labor unions but instead revolve around the dynamics of the capitalist economy and the activities of the dominant economic elite. Nevertheless, some people will disregard this and continue to decry the irrelevance of labor unions as a force for economic justice, suggesting they under-mine productivity and hurt individual companies, as if this proves that they're a drag on the larger economy.

To respond to any of this we need to answer a few questions, such as, what do we mean by "productivity" and what is the impact of a labor union in a workplace? To be clear, "productivity" has a formal meaning in the context of work that is different from the way you or I might use it in everyday discussion. This is actually something that got me into trouble years ago when I first served on a union negotiating team representing my coworkers. I thought of "productivity" as, essentially, "being productive," that is, creating good, quality work and not wasting time. I was mistaken.

In the economy, productivity refers to the output from a pro-duction or work process per hour based on given inputs. It comes down to how much, per hour, a worker is able to produce. Productiv-ity can change based on the use or non-use of technology, the skill level of given workers, the amount of training, the age of the work-force, or any number of other factors including wages/salaries.

In general, the employer wants to put as little into the produc-tion of anything to maximize productivity and their profits. Some-times it works out, but occasionally employers find that putting too little in reaps little payoff. It's also important to keep in mind that at least when it comes to business, the employer class prioritizes its particular needs rather than social needs, or looking out for the common good. At the same time, and particularly when facing op-ponents from among working people, they tend to develop clear consciousness as a class.

Think, for a moment, about baseball. Team owners want ex-ceptional athletes and value skilled hitters and pitchers, but play-ers aren't born that way; they must be groomed. This grooming was achieved largely by starting players early with sandlot baseball and little league teams until eventually you got to the level of minor league or farm teams. The owners needed little league teams to have candidates for the minor leagues, and they needed minor league teams to have candidates for the major league teams.

At the same time, baseball has always been a global industry. Players would come to the United States especially from Puerto Rico, Cuba, the Dominican Republic, and Mexico. And, truth be told, American players would often migrate outside the country to play ball, even on a temporary basis. Nevertheless, over the last forty years owners have increasingly relied on the global trade of players, making it less necessary to invest domestically in the requisite training that any player needs. Despite the impact on domestic nonprofessional baseball and the options available for young men, team owners think at the level of their bottom line and seek to reduce costs and concerns so that they can gain maximum advantage.

We'll return to this question of the impact of unions on productivity in a moment, but it's worth asking an obvious if problematic question: Who should benefit from improvements in productivity?

From the standpoint of right-wing libertarians, who view the world of work as if it were a feudal fiefdom where everything is to be controlled by the owner or employer, the answer is simple: employers should benefit. As one right-wing libertarian argued with me on a radio talk show, each company has an owner who should be able to do what he or she wants! But, consider this: companies don't exist in isolation. Banks lend money and governments offer varying forms of support for companies, including zoning, security, and tax advantages. But on top of all of this, the company would be nowhere without a workforce.[19] It's the workforce that generates the product, whether a material product, for example, such as a car, or an intellectual product, such as software or research. Therefore, when workers are more economically productive, they're laying the foundation for an increase in the employer's profits.

Early on labor unions recognized a basic issue of fairness was at stake: if workers were producing the wealth, then they should be entitled to a share. A basic assumption entered into worker/employer relations in most Western capitalist countries that held that if productivity goes up, the workers should gain a share of that, usually through wage and benefit improvements. Following

World War II, this assumption was widely accepted and influenced many non-union companies that feared that if they didn't match what many unionized companies offered, they too would become unionized.

This assumption began to change in the late 1970s, and by the Reagan Revolution of the 1980s, it had changed dramatically. It did not change on its own but was part of an orchestrated political and ideological effort that helped exacerbate the wealth polarization. These myths, including the notion of the rugged individual, who, allegedly, had made it on his own, propagated. But the assumption was also deeply rooted in the notion of private property— specifically, private ownership—and who should be considered the owner. Beginning with the Reagan era, the individual entrepreneur was esteemed as the source of new wealth and creativity, while the working person came to be viewed as, at best, a well-placed tool in the hands of a great craftsperson (the entrepreneur). During this moment, the notion that unions had a positive role in the economy was challenged. An increasing chorus began to insist that unions undermined productivity, thereby hurting the competitiveness of the economy. For many, this assertion became the truth, but the actual situation is far more complex.

Various studies have asserted, and have established, that labor unions play either a neutral or a positive role in productivity. These include a 1982 study by Kim Clark, *Unionization and Firm Performance*, and a 2004 study by Hristos Doucouliagos and Patrice Laroche, *The Impact of U.S. Unions on Productivity*. In the former study, Clark concludes that unionized and non-unionized firms in the same industry differ only in their profitability, while productivity, growth, and the capital-labor ratio among firms prove to be roughly the same.[20] Doucouliagos and Laroche conclude that "all the available evidence indicates that unions have a positive and statistically significant positive effect on productivity in U.S. manufacturing and education, of 10 percent and 7 percent, respectively. However, given that U.S. unions appear to increase wages by around 15 percent . . . there is a net negative impact on profitability."[21]

In a separate paper, Harley Shaiken, writing for the Center for American Progress, noted, "The economics literature points to the fact that unionization and high productivity are certainly compatible . . . Brown and Medoff . . . found in looking at manufacturing industries that 'unionized establishments are about 22 percent more productive than those that are not.' In much of the postwar period, this higher productivity underwrote the higher wages that unions were able to win."[22]

Ironically, a paper from the World Bank (not known for being at the vanguard of workers' rights) has findings that are not dissimilar from the above papers. In their book *Unions and Collective Bargaining*, Toke Aidt and Zafiris Tzannatos note that the economic impact of unions on economic performance other than wages is less understood. A range of factors influence results, including the country itself and the extent of unionization. Interestingly, though the paper came from the World Bank, there was no across-the-board condemnation of unions when it came to productivity, but there were issues about company profitability.[23]

All right, so let's try to make some sense out of this. First, leaving aside ideologues who smear unions, there is no consensus that unions hurt productivity. Rather, it appears that either they assist it or that their impact is neutral. In fact, studies also indicate that contrary to common myths, unions don't generally inhibit the introduction of new technology. Instead, they bargain over the terms of such technology and the consequences of their introduction. In the building trades, actually, unionization has clearly had a significant and positive impact on productivity. The Mechanical Contractors Association in Chicago noted, "Union workers receive extensive training and so incur fewer injuries and lawsuits. Their quality workmanship results in greater productivity and timely results, and that adds up to savings."[24]

But what about this issue of profitability? What this really is about is that unions, by definition, attempt to ensure that workers get a share of the profits, that is, that they—the workers—gain from productivity increases a company may obtain. In that sense, a company without a union is dominated by an individual or group that seeks to maximize the wealth *they* obtain from what workers produce. A union, as a countervailing force, seeks to distribute more fairly the results of the labor of the workers. Therefore, when you see something in the newspaper that says that a union hurts profitability, this does not necessarily mean what the media is asking you to believe. It is not saying that the union is driving the company out of business, but rather it is probably saying that the union wants to make sure that the workers receive a better bargain for all they put into bringing about the company's profits. Again, this comes down to confronting an important myth: whether the entrepreneur or the worker creates the profits. The mainstream media would have you believe it's the former, whereas reality proves otherwise.

When conservative, anti-worker pundits suggest that unions are bankrupting us, they aren't standing on firm ground; they're attempting to create a scapegoat for a much deeper economic problem that's on a scale way beyond what unions could create. But the bias in reporting takes us back to Galbraith's notion that understanding capitalism means that you must recognize that the controlling force in such a society represents capital. Further, those representing capital perceive that any impediment—real or imagined—to the further accumulation of profits is antagonistic to the interests of that society.

"UNIONS ARE ACTUALLY RUN BY 'LABOR BOSSES,' AREN'T THEY?"

In most mainstream media outlets, newspapers or otherwise, writers will almost invariably use one of two terms when speaking about the leadership of labor unions: "labor boss" or "union boss." It has become so common over the years that mainstream writers don't seem to understand that the very terms are problematic. Just to take one small example, consider this headline from the online *Silicon Valley Mercury News*: "Sports Digest: NFL Commissioner, Labor Boss Make Joint Appearance."[1] Yet for most of these same writers, it would be inconceivable that they would refer to the president of the United States as the boss of the United States. So, what about this term?

WHAT IS A "LABOR BOSS"?

Regardless of the writer's intention, use of these terms brings at least two things to mind—the first is that of organized crime, addressed later, and the second is a presumption of the dictatorship of one individual (or clique) over the entire union organization. For a deeper understanding, we have to look at how unions operate so we can appreciate, first, why these terms are biased and unhelpful, and, second, identify some real challenges that *do* take place within unions that many people, including pro-union people, often try to sweep under the rug.

HOW DO UNIONS OPERATE?

Unions are structured along a particular hierarchy. At the base, there's a "local union" that individuals join. The local union, which normally has a number identifying it, that is, Local 1985, may also have a name, but it is typically known by the number. It is responsible, in most cases, for issues that affect workers in a given workplace. Its size can range from a few dozen to thousands depending on the union itself. It may or may not be responsible for negotiating a contract (a collective bargaining agreement that outlines the terms and conditions of employment agreed to by the workers and the employer) with a particular employer, but that largely depends on whether, for example, there is a very large employer, say, General Motors, with plants all over the country. If there is a very large employer, there may be a "master agreement" (which covers the major items that would affect all the workers working in different facilities of the same company) with the company, along with "supplemental agreements" for the specific plants (where details are handled that address the specifics of a given facility). Again, this depends on the industry and company. Also, a local union may represent workers at several different companies in a specific geographical area, sometimes in the same industry and sometimes not.

Above the local union may be a regional or district body that represents many states, and which may have significance or be virtually irrelevant. It may be a body that joins together several local unions in the same geographic area, negotiates contracts, and provides representational assistance. Or it may help mainly to coordinate certain common projects, such as legislative and/or electoral activity.

There's also the *national union*, or what is often called the *international union*. The term "international union" goes back to the nineteenth century when US-based unions began organizing outside the country. They moved into Canada and, in the early twentieth century, attempted to organize in the Caribbean. These efforts stopped for various reasons, but because these US-based unions were not confined to this country, they were known as "internationals."[2] Most "internationals" are composed of workers from the United States and its territories and may have an autonomous Canadian component.

The national or international union is composed of the local unions. The national/international holds a convention normally every three to four years where the leadership is chosen and major decisions are made. The convention is composed of delegates chosen by and from the local unions based on their membership. There is usually a formula that might go something like this: for every X hundred *paid* members, the union receives Y number delegates. Thus, the larger the paid membership, the greater the number of delegates a local union will hold at the convention.

The leadership of a union is chosen through an election. Let's look first at the local union. Normally, elections are held on the basis of one member, one vote. A nomination process is established, and the election takes place on a predetermined day. The election is normally for the top officers, which include the president, secretary-treasurer (who oversees the finances and the basic administration), and in some cases some other officers. There is also an executive board, which may be elected at the same time or may be constituted by local union representatives called *shop stewards* (workers chosen to represent their coworkers in a specific area of a workplace to make sure that members are organized and that the contract is enforced).

Depending on the size of the local union, the elected leaders may choose to *hire* an individual to oversee the day-to-day operations of the organization. This person may be called the executive director or general manager. It is important to be aware of this, because many of the elected officers of the local union continue to work full-time and can only do union work on the job when there is a contractual agreement with the employer that permits time away from work for union business. Otherwise, these individuals do their union work "off the clock" (and frequently for no pay). It is largely for that reason that an individual may be chosen to operate the union on a day-to-day basis.[3]

At the national/international level, the top or general officers are often elected at the convention. In some very rare cases, officers are chosen by a vote of the membership as a whole, such as with the International Brotherhood of Teamsters. If chosen at the convention, it is based on delegates voting. So, while a candidate may, prior to the convention, visit different parts of the United States (and Canada, Puerto Rico, and some other locales) if appropriate, at the end of the day, the individuals who will actually be doing the voting will be the delegates to the convention. When these delegates vote, depending on the constitution of the union, they may or may not be voting based on decisions of the local union. In other words, a local union may pledge its votes to a particular candidate or there may be a case where the local union is split over what candidate to endorse.[4]

UNIONS AS POLITICAL ORGANIZATIONS

What is important to gather from this is that, as opposed to a corporation, unions are political organizations in the sense that leadership is elected and there is membership engagement in the process. The extent of that membership engagement, however, varies from union to union.

For these reasons, the notion of a union or labor "boss" is not useful and is, in effect, defamatory. It disregards the basic fact that there's an electoral process within unions and that, even when the process doesn't work well—and we shall discuss that below—there is *nothing comparable in corporate America.*

Optimally, a union member, if they choose to get involved with their local union, has an opportunity through meetings and voting, to participate in the life of the union. Many members choose not to get involved, however. They may not have the time; they may feel the union is irrelevant to the rest of their life; or there may be obstacles within the union that discourage their participation. The point here, before we proceed, is to understand that in most cases there are opportunities for democratic involvement.

That said, why does the term "union boss" or "labor boss" stick around? It's not simply due to the power of the propaganda by anti-worker media, though this is a *very* important factor. There are two other reasons. One, most people have no clue how unions function. They read the press or watch television and assume what they hear is correct. They are led to believe that unions are huge organizations comparable to corporations, so they arrived at certain conclusions.

As a union member and supporter, I wish I could stop there, but the reality is that deep-seated problems also exist within the union movement itself. Here are a few examples.

Because of the (elected) delegate process in union elections (at the national/international level), the power to influence convention elections is found at the level of the local union leadership. This means that if you happen not to be in the favor of the local union leadership, your voice may not be heard (unless you have organized a significant enough constituency such that you cannot be ignored).

There are other potential problems. The top leadership of most unions, by having access to resources, can hold those as a "trump card" over the head of a local union. For instance, let's say that your union is facing a major fight with an employer. Perhaps your union is relatively small or perhaps it just doesn't have the level of resources to conduct a struggle. So, you go to the national/international and ask for support. In the best of all possible worlds, the national/international leadership will evaluate the situation objectively and give support because of that evaluation. But that doesn't always happen. In some cases, a decision may be based on whether the leadership of your local has been supportive of the national/international's leadership. The reverse can also be true, for instance, if your local crossed the national/international leadership, your local may not receive the sort of support it needs.

Nothing should be surprising about these scenarios. They play themselves out regularly in our political arena. Yet, because unions are supposed to be workers' organizations and actively fighting for fairness and justice, they are held, rightly or wrongly, to a different standard. As a result, when there's an exposure of undemocratic or corrupt conduct, this flies in the face of the stated purpose of labor unions. The mainstream, pro-corporate media then often uses such examples as a means of disparaging unions and unionism itself.

There are at least two other aspects to this issue. The dynamics of employer/worker relations often encourages a militaristic or corporate approach on the part of union leaders. Think of it this way: if someone is regularly out to get you, you'll be on the defensive and often quite suspicious. You'll be anticipating attacks and will act accordingly. As the saying goes, "Just because you're paranoid, doesn't mean that someone isn't out to get you."

The rise of trade unionism did not happen peacefully. In general, employers took every step they could to crush any level of self-organization of workers. As a result, unions often needed very strong leadership and tight organization to withstand repression. This led to a situation in many unions where dissent was treated as disloyalty in the face of the "enemy." This is completely understandable on the one hand, and equally destructive on the other. In these circumstances, instead of a robust debate, factions regularly emerged (sometimes looking like and acting like political parties), and loyalty to one or another faction became one's ticket, if not one's identity. In fact, it is true to this day that in certain unions an inner core holds power, and those who challenge this core are seen as undermining the unity of the union.

Another factor that has influenced the lack of democracy in some unions is that too many unions attempt to emulate the employers. A phenomenon of what came to be known as "business unionism" emerged in the late nineteenth century. Instead of being understood as a workers' organization fighting for economic justice, the union came to be seen in some quarters as a counterpart to the employer, operating like and often resembling a business. The leaders of the local union wanted to be treated as equal to the employer, so in some cases they sought high salaries and other benefits to demonstrate to the employer, the members, and the world that they should be treated with and deserve the same respect as the employers.[5] Indeed, the members often wanted their leaders to dress and live like the employers, as if this gave them—the workers—more power.

Because of this, union leaders started to live markedly different lives from their members. It became so different that the thought of returning to the workplace became inconceivable and, as a result, they did what they could to hold on to power. Most unions lack term limits, so it was quite possible for someone to be elected and, through the power of the incumbency, retain power for years, if not decades. Such a situation turns democracy into nothing more than a formality, at best.

It is important to be clear that nothing stated here suggests that all or even most unions lack democracy. The challenge concerning democracy is one that faces all unions and, for that matter, all political organizations (including nation-states). Many unions have addressed issues of internal democracy through their election processes, internal education, as well as in their culture of internal debate. Nevertheless, the flag of caution must always fly.

Over the years, there have been organizations that have worked with union members to fight for democracy and against corruption. These have included the New York–based Association for Union Democracy,[6] the Detroit-based *Labor Notes* magazine,[7] and the North Carolina–based Black Workers for Justice,[8] as well as myriad rank-and-file pro-democracy caucuses and organizations within unions, with the Teamsters for a Democratic Union[9] among the most prominent.

What conclusions can we draw from this? The most important is that in any political organization there are both opportunities as well as dangers when it comes to democracy. There are no structural guarantees for democracy. There are structural mechanisms, such as term limits and reasonable restraints on officer salaries, that can inhibit toxic practices. But the most effective counter to undemocratic practices rests in an educated and active membership. When the membership of any organization—or country for that matter—is lulled to sleep, not encouraged to participate, or chooses not to participate, the danger of tyranny becomes a real threat.

Sections of the mainstream media, along with right-wing opponents of unions, have seized on undemocratic practices where they exist to disparage unions with the brush that paints all or most union leaders as "labor bosses." Ironically, one rarely hears major employers described in the media as "corporate bosses," or other such terms. In fact, over the years, no matter what one may think about a particular owner or employer, they are normally referred to in the mainstream media as "chief executive officer" or, in other cases, "chairperson of the board of directors," this despite the fact that corporations do not even put up the pretense of being democratic organizations. When it comes to workers' organization, however, such respect is noticeably lacking from the mainstream or elite media.

The use of the term "labor boss" is a way of dismissively describing workers as riffraff. It also serves to portray the union leader as a de facto if not de jure dictator. It is aimed at bringing to mind an organization that is mindless except for a manipulative leader directing a faceless mass of people. Thus, in using the term, one gets absolutely the wrong impression of the workings of a labor union as well as some of the problems that can arise within them. In fact, and to return to an earlier point, the continuous disparaging of labor unions, including but not limited to the use of terms such as "labor boss," can lead to a defensiveness on the part of labor union members when it comes to any degree of criticism. All criticism becomes suspect because it is all too often associated with being a weapon to destroy the organization that workers built. As a result, actual problems can be covered up for fear of airing dirty laundry.

"PUBLIC SECTOR UNIONS CAUSE BUDGET DEFICITS, RIGHT?"

Since the 1980s, public sector unions have found themselves under assault largely by right-wing think tanks and conservative politicians. These attacks have employed the same coded language, for instance, "public sector unions hurt government functioning." But the form of the attacks was largely indirect in that politicians did not seek to eliminate public sector unions from the scene but rather reduce the funding for government in general (beginning with the antitax revolts of the 1970s). The right of collective bargaining for public sector workers was generally not attacked directly—except in the South and Southwest—but public sector workers were increasingly challenged.

The forms of the attacks on public sector workers were most often variants of privatization. Particularly in the Reagan era, the myth that "private sector can do it better" was promulgated and repeated so often that many liberals and even some progressives accepted it as true. Privatization and subcontracting became a means for allegedly saving costs and getting work done more efficiently. Unfortunately, not even the facts to the contrary could undermine many of these ideologically driven arguments.

Before getting into the meat of the challenge to public sector unionism, let's take a moment to point out the problem with the anti–public sector myths. What mythmakers ignore are those facts that undermine their core argument. For instance, I once had a discussion with a very wealthy Republican who contended that the private sector always did things better than the public sector. I asked him about the New York City subway system and how it began. He was perplexed by my question until I pointed out that the system began as a private sector venture, but the private sector couldn't sustain it and it, in fact, went bankrupt. I indicated that this has happened in countless ventures, and the formula is almost always the same: the private sector does what it does until it goes bankrupt and then it looks to the public sector for help. Not much for taking risks.

This rich individual actually had no response and proceeded to change the subject. This regularly plays out in political circles, and I need to acknowledge that many Democrats, particularly those influenced by the Democratic Leadership Council (a more conservative wing of the Democratic Party, formed in the mid-1980s), have also bought into this rhetoric.

The bottom line is that the public sector is both the guarantor of last resort as well as the provider of facilities and resources that have a broader social need and constituency than can be provided by any *one* private sector entity. Because of this, they can't operate on the same basis as a private sector entity. They aren't constructed to make a maximum profit, nor can they be. For example, think about the US Postal Service. The USPS guarantees that a package can be sent and received for a given cost anywhere in the United States. If you send an envelope first class, it'll cost the same whether it's sent from Boston, Massachusetts, or Boise, Idaho. Imagine, then, what happens if mail traffic is privatized. Various studies indicate that the price between certain major metropolitan areas would drop due to the mail flow, while the cost to rural Montana would skyrocket. Fundamentally, this is all about different priorities, and whether citizens and residents have certain guarantees or should be subject to the whims of the market.

WHAT ABOUT PUBLIC SECTOR UNIONS?

Public sector unions were illegal in most states, cities, and, indeed, the federal government for a long time. They emerged slowly in the early twentieth century, and in most places first as *associations*. Even when they called themselves unions in places where collective bargaining and unions were illegal, they functioned as supportive organizations for their members. In some cases, these organizations operated as professional associations to raise the stature and importance of the particular field, like teaching. In still other cases, such as the National Alliance of Postal and Federal Employees (NAPFE), these associations and proto-unions also functioned as advocacy groups for specific constituencies. In the case of the NAPFE, African American workers faced significant racial discrimination in the postal system and federal government in the early through mid-twentieth century.

Over the course of the twentieth century, public sector unionism emerged as a significant current. In many respects, its rise can be tied to the fight against corruption and cronyism in the public sector. Prior to the introduction of public sector unions and certainly prior to the civil service, the public sector was a reservoir for patronage positions. With little to guide the selection of the workforce, racial, ethnic, and gender discrimination were major features of public sector employment, not to mention outright payoffs for jobs. Public sector unions became an important instrument in overcoming this corruption and favoritism by winning procedures that became standard protocols, including hiring and termination processes. But public sector unionism was also an important mechanism, and indeed a movement, which was instrumental in raising the living standards of those who dedicated themselves to public service.

It's important to note that financial support for the organizing of public sector workers came from the private sector unions, which saw the public sector as needing to be organized if the victories that had been won in the private sector were to survive. Public sector unions owe private sector unions a major debt of gratitude for this support.

Particularly with the rise of a new, energized unionism in the 1930s, public sector unions became part of the social landscape, albeit slower in their rise than the then-new private sector unions. Only in 1961, however, were unions fully permitted in the federal sector as a result of an executive order by President John F. Kennedy. But collective bargaining in the federal sector did not start until the 1970s. Over the course of the decades, increasing numbers of states introduced variants on collective bargaining for public sector employees. Many states in the South and Southwest continue to prohibit collective bargaining for public sector workers. This is, in large part, a legacy of the extremely repressive, racist, and anti-worker policies that permeated the South and the Southwest from the era of slavery and the Civil War (for the South) and from the annexation of the Southwest from Mexico. In these regions, efforts to bring workers together across racial/ethnic boundaries were repressed, and efforts at economic justice generally were repressed by political regimes that supported the domination of both landowners and the developing manufacturing sector. In light of this, any form of public sector unionism was antithetical to the climate that these political and economic elites were prepared to tolerate. There are, however, sometimes arrangements for what are called "memoranda of understanding" between a public sector union and a governmental body that amounts to informal agreements between the parties.

What public sector unions are able to do largely depends on the collective bargaining laws mandated by that state. Keep in mind that public sector collective bargaining is *not* determined by the National Labor Relations Act (NLRA): it's determined by state laws, which is why it varies (or, in the federal sector, by the Federal Labor Relations Act).

That said, there are a few general points that can be made about public sector unionism:

1. Federal sector unionism and nonfederal sector public unionism are markedly different. In the federal sector, there's a prohibition against bargaining over wages and benefits. This arena has been granted to Congress.

2. Public sector unions (of employees at the state, county, and municipal levels)—where there is collective bargaining—normally may bargain over wages, hours, and working conditions. The extent to which the union may bargain over any of these things will be dictated by state law.

3. Public sector unions in the United States are generally denied the right to strike. If they choose to strike anyway, there are severe penalties imposed by courts.

4. In the absence of the right to strike, binding "interest arbitration" exists in many cases. The idea is that an independent third party reviews the final bargaining position of both sides and then *imposes* a settlement (which may be either of the proposals or some combination of those offered by the parties, depending on the parameters given to the arbitrator).

Before turning to the federal sector, I want to reiterate two points. First, the right to public sector bargaining and unionism means that the workers have to decide whether they wish to have a union in the first place.

The second, and perhaps most important, point is that the mere existence of a public sector union doesn't affect a state, county, or municipal budget. In fact, bargaining only affects the budget in one way: it guarantees that budget decisions that affect public employees aren't unilateral. Where there is binding interest arbitration, a neutral third party evaluates the proposals of both sides and makes the final decision.

As we saw in the case of Wisconsin in early 2011, the Republican governor, Scott Walker, alleged that weakening public sector unions was in the public's interest and would save money. This, of course, after he offered tax breaks to the rich and the corporations.[1] In practice, the only way that "weakening" public sector unions saves money is by diminishing the power of unions to argue on behalf of their members. In other words, if you exclude certain matters from collective bargaining, such as health care, or if you organizationally weaken unions, for instance, through eliminating dues deduction (that is, the right to have dues taken out of one's check and submitted to the union), then you are opting for unilaterally imposed decisions rather than anything approaching genuine negotiations.

For some this might sound fair, because it's often presented as being in the taxpayer's interests—such as Governor Walker's suggestion that forcing unions to win annual recertification somehow addresses the state's budget crisis—but it must be stressed that the decision favors wealthy taxpayers. Weakening public sector unions by eliminating their right to bargain allows political leaders to ignore the question of revenue. That is, the political leaders, like many employers, can seek to reduce costs by gouging the workforce rather than turning to those who have accrued vast sums of money. This is at the heart of the so-called budgetary crisis. With decreasing weight given to taxing wealth and the wealthy, the political establishment has focused on extracting as much as they can from those at the bottom—at least the bottom 90 percent.

There is also a very basic question. The political Right—in arguing that the wages and benefits of public sector workers comes at the expense of the taxpayers—are arguing, in effect, that public sector workers should not receive compensation that helps them live. Of course, the wages and benefits come out of taxes. The point is that the revenue stream should be organized in such a way that it is fair, rather than pressing down on those who can least afford to pay it. The other factor is that public sector workers are doing a service—their job—for the larger society. Is this something for which they should receive inadequate compensation? If so, what are the ramifications for the quality of the workforce, not to mention the quality of the work performed?

Republicans aren't the only ones who have moved against public sector unions. To the shock of so many in Massachusetts,

Illinois, New Jersey, and Connecticut, Democratic Party legislators took steps in 2011 to weaken unions, allegedly in the name of cost-cutting.[2] In virtually every case, public sector unions have been blamed as if they're the source of the fiscal woes of states, counties, and municipalities. The reality is that public sector unions are being crushed because political elites perceive them as being obstacles to addressing fiscal dilemmas. In the absence of a strong organized workforce, political elites can impose their will and ignore questions about tax policy and new sources of revenue.

Let's analyze this a little more deeply. Public sector unions tend to bring with them an improvement in the wages and benefits of public sector workers.[3] There is no reason for unions to be apologetic for this. If unions were not raising the living standard of those they represent, there would be no reason for their existence.

A 2003 study out of North Carolina State University arrived at interesting conclusions regarding public sector unions.

> Public sector unions do not have a significant impact on government productivity one way or the other, but they may push for more government services and workers. Public sector unions have been moderately successful in improving the wages of government workers, especially those at the lower reaches of the wage scale, and even more so the non-wage benefits of these workers. These unions have been leaders in the fight for comparable pay regardless of gender or race.[4]

In other words, public sector unions serve to lift public sector workers out of near or actual poverty-level conditions and fight for more equity within the workforce. The fact that they push for more government services and a larger workforce isn't indicative of featherbedding, wherein bogus jobs are created. Rather, the union acts as an advocate for a better and more effective labor force.

To be precise, the wage difference between state workers under collective bargaining compared with those without is about $5,883 annually. In 2006, the average state worker's salary nationwide was

$43,875, not exactly the salary of yacht owners.[5] These figures are noteworthy because they contradict the popular assumption that public sector workers have been living a privileged life. With salaries averaging around $44,000 in 2006, and since having undergone a major recession, along with budget cuts, layoffs, and wage freezes, it would be difficult to imagine that there has been much improvement.

Unions exist to fight for improvements in the lives of those they represent, regardless of whether they're members. They will, by definition, push their employers—agency directors and elected officials—to improve the conditions for those who offer public service. There's nothing in the existence of the union, however, that mandates that what they ask for they must receive. This is what makes the narrative from the extreme Right so completely disingenuous. If you take their arguments to their logical conclusion, it'd be as if someone claimed that the existence of lobbyists increased the costs for governments! Lobbyists operate in the interests of their clients or employers. In a best-case scenario, a lobbyist is trying to make a governmental body aware of something that they may not have considered or that they de-prioritized. In other cases, the lobbyist is trying to pressure the governmental body or elected official to move in a direction they might not have otherwise considered.

A public sector union is, for all intents and purposes, a mass lobby. They are a collective advocate for those they represent. Efforts to weaken them, therefore, are designed to remove their point of view—that of the public employee—from any discussion. What makes the public sector union a unique lobby is that, when it is at its best, it is an advocate for the public interest and not simply for the interests of its own members, that is, advocating for the number of students in a classroom, or for increasing the size of environmental protection agencies.

Attacks on federal sector unions have an even more bizarre twist. Federal sector unions are denied the right to bargain over wages and benefits. In fact, the scope of bargaining is far narrower than outside of the federal sector.[6] They can, however, bargain over certain conditions of work, schedules, grievance procedures, and other areas, but the narrowness of the list makes it that much more difficult for unions in the federal sector. In addition to the narrowness of bargaining, the entire federal sector is "open shop," meaning federal sector unions must represent all workers irrespective of whether they're members.

The wages and benefits that federal workers receive are decided by Congress. Of course, federal sector unions lobby Congress, but so, too, do groups that oppose the objectives of federal sector unions. Therefore, it's a matter of democracy or the lack thereof whether federal sector unions should be allowed to voice the concerns of the workers they represent. The mere existence of federal sector unions, then, doesn't bring about any significant increase in costs for the federal government.

One of the attacks against federal sector unions is on something that most people have never heard about: "official time." Official time is time granted per the Federal Labor Relations Act (FLRA) for a union to perform the duty of representing workers. It's actually very straightforward: federal sector unions are obligated by law to represent all workers in certified bargaining units, regardless of whether they're members. Further, the federal sector unions can't require payment from nonmembers for representational services, or they risk being charged with an "unfair labor practice" and face significant ramifications.

Official time means that the union representative can take time off from their regular job duties to represent the worker. The union representative can also take time off to conduct contract negotiations. They can't take time off, however, to lobby Congress or to organize other workers.

Some right-wing politicians have alleged that official time represents an unwarranted cost for the taxpayers to pick up. This amounts to demagoguery. If a union is obligated to represent *all* workers in a given bargaining unit (and if all those workers are not paying any sort of service fee), the union faces significant costs.

Representation isn't just about grievances, but it also involves looking out for the well-being of the entire bargaining unit, without regard to union membership. If these politicians are really concerned about costs, they could ensure that nonmembers paid a fee (an "agency fee" in the nonfederal sector) to defray the costs of representation. No such proposal will emerge, however, because the attacks don't concern costs in the narrow sense of the term, but rather concern the very existence of organizations that represent working people.

Let's think about it for a moment. The right wing says that the taxpayers are paying for the unions. That is actually not the case. What they are doing is paying for time for representation. In that sense, it is similar to government providing legal aid attorneys to individuals who cannot afford their own. The government is ensuring that someone gets proper representation even if they have no funds to afford one. In this case, the taxpayers are ensuring that federal workers, irrespective of union membership, have the right to be represented. That means that *someone* has to represent them.

Therefore, it's important to understand that the myth concerning public sector unions allegedly raising costs and threatening budgets doesn't conform to reality. The real objective in going after public sector unions is to eliminate the voice of working people and to weaken their ability to significantly participate in political and legislative action that challenges the wealthy. It's truly the golden rule as far as the political elite are concerned: whoever holds the gold—in this case, the major share of society's wealth—rules. And they are not particularly interested in sharing.

"UNIONS MAKE UNREASONABLE DEMANDS THAT RESULT IN LOTS OF STRIKES!"

The claim that unions make unreasonable demands has been around since unions first emerged. The fundamental question one has to consider is actually quite simple: *what is unreasonable?* To answer this question you have to remember: *workers and employers do not have the same interests.*[1] This doesn't mean that their interests are always and in every case antagonistic; simply that their interests aren't the same.

Recognizing these contradictory interests undermines many of the economic myths that suggest that everyone is an equal player if they work for the same company or governmental body. But your everyday experience tells you exactly the opposite. It's not as simple as differences in wages or that employers and employees often live in different communities or drive different sorts of cars. Rather, it has to do with what happens in the workplace that any worker can feel, irrespective of their individual, one-on-one relationship with any given employer.

Because of these different conditions, workers spontaneously conclude that they need to organize. That organization may or may not be a union; it may be something completely ad hoc, responding to very particular conditions. Or it might be something longer term, such as a labor union.

The demands that workers make through their unions are, generally, demands that speak to a particular set of needs they face. The demands may also speak to a desire for fairness and equity at work, which can be both vis-à-vis other workers (i.e., challenging favoritism carried out by the employer) or against the employer.

As noted earlier, employers capture a portion of the wealth created by the workers and workers believe they are receiving compensation, fair or otherwise, for what they have produced.

Now related to this is that on the basis of both what the employer captures from the worker (in the private sector) and the profits they are able to gain through the sale of the product, they enrich themselves. In the United States, as with most capitalist societies, this is considered fair by the elite. From the standpoint of the elite, it's reasonable that they pay as little as possible for workers to produce because, after all, they—the employers—own the company. In contrast, the union focuses on redistributing the surplus.

This means that there are very different ideas about justice depending on where you stand. If you believe that you should control all "your" profits and hand out what you want for the people who work for you, then *any* demand to redistribute the wealth will be perceived as "unreasonable." On the other hand, if you believe that you are working hard under very difficult conditions and that your good work is enriching someone else, you'll believe that demands for redistribution are reasonable and just. In this sense, it needs to be clear that there is no objective definition of what is reasonable—as far as demands—and what's unreasonable: it all depends on both the conditions under which the demands are made and on which side of the economic line you happen to be.

The employer class and their media allies often make the demands presented by workers seem outrageous. Yet historically, certain demands that were once portrayed as outrageous, in time became common sense. One example of this is the area of health and safety.

As a former shipyard worker I can tell you that in the mid-1970s, health and safety protection for the average worker, shipyard or otherwise, wasn't taken for granted. To argue in favor of basic health and safety led many a shipyard worker to be accused of being "weak," or a "coward." The demand for basic worker protection was often ignored and portrayed as being unreasonable, expensive, and detrimental to profits. Putting extra planking to prevent dangerous falls was seen as unnecessary, and even some union leaders thought that the demand for healthy and safe working conditions often went overboard. In 1978, I was working in a shipyard and fell twenty feet. A week before, someone had fallen nine feet and had died from his injuries. I survived only because I was knocked unconscious on the way down. As soon as it was reported that I had fallen, workers were immediately sent to the area where I was lying to place additional planking that should've been there in the first place. Today you can still find this practice, for instance, in the mining industry, the most dangerous in the country.[2]

As someone who has negotiated many contracts, I haven't encountered many instances of "unreasonable" demands. What I have encountered is what could be described as one's *initial bargaining position(s) or demands.* There's nothing particularly unusual about this since it isn't different from any other bargaining situation. For example, let's say you want to buy a house that is going for $X. The average cost of similar houses in that location is $X minus $30,000, and your starting offer is $X minus $80,000. Who is unreasonable in this scenario depends on your point of view. One might not agree to the terms; one might conclude that the other side is asking too much; or both sides might describe the other side as "unreasonable" because their interests are different. It's all part of the bargaining process. Both sides can walk away, and in walking away, either side might reconsider their position.

Recall any experience where you've negotiated or bargained, and you'll realize it's all about point of view. In that sense, "unreasonable" is rhetorical and contextual. At one point, the emancipation of slaves was considered "unreasonable," at least from the standpoint of slave owners, while slaves believed emancipation was an essential moral and practical necessity.

You, the observer, then have to ask whether any set of demands are reasonable or unreasonable. Is it unreasonable to want a salary or wage on which you can live? Is it unreasonable to want benefits so you can cover health-care and education/training costs for your family? Is it unreasonable to want a safe and healthy workplace rather than facing the prospect of incapacitating injuries or illnesses? Is it unreasonable to gain a larger share of the surplus given the work that you put into the job?

Let's take this a little further to unpack a distinctly American perspective. In this country, there's a tendency to make comments like this: "If I do not have X, Y, or Z, then no one should have it." This doesn't mean that people don't want to improve their lives. Rather it means that people are often manipulated by charlatans who prey on jealousy, envy, despair, and resentment to the detriment of those at the bottom.

We can see this all around us. For instance, in this time of employer takeaways, when people are losing pensions, demagogues will tap into the resentment that many people feel about this situation but target it at those who still have pensions. So, rather than concluding that everyone needs a pension, the argument follows that those who have them, that is, public sector workers, should give them up to be like everyone else! This is generally called the "crabs in the barrel syndrome." In fact, so much of bargaining in recent times has been *concessionary* precisely due to this sort of climate; employers yell that they cannot pay or offer certain benefits, claiming that no one else gets this pay and benefits and, therefore, the workers who have them should relinquish them.

Most demands for the improvement of one's condition, or in many cases a defense of what one has against an onslaught of "takeaways," are regularly defined by the economic elite as being unreasonable. The elite challenge such demands because they tend to shatter the status quo. Once won, such demands can spread and gain support. This has nothing to do with whether abstractly the demand is reasonable or unreasonable, but rather, if the demand is perceived as a threat to the common interests of the employer class.

Therefore, when someone accuses labor unions of being unreasonable, it's important to dissect the allegation. What are the demands? Do they seem to be addressing a real problem? Do the proposed solutions seem to make sense? Are there other options the union could've advanced? How different are those options? How do their demands compare with the working conditions, pay, and benefit levels of the top corporate officers?

The second part of the allegation concerns strikes. To make any sense of this, let's understand what a strike is and why it has historically been used by workers to make their point. It's also worth considering the question of strikes in today's context.

Simply put, a strike is a cessation of work called by the workers. A strike is a work stoppage, but a work stoppage isn't necessarily a strike. There are different types of work stoppages, including those carried out by employers (called "lockouts"). A strike can take any number of forms—it may be the result of intense planning, or it may be spontaneous.

There are famous strikes, such as those that took place in 1877 primarily in the Northeast and Midwest that were focused on railroads. There were the general strikes (strikes in which everyone, regardless of a specific union or non-union type of job—from secretary to nurse to retail worker to electrician to factory worker—refuses to go to work) that took place in 1934 in the San Francisco Bay area; in Toledo, Ohio; and in Minneapolis. In 1934, there was also the famous nationwide textile strike (though largely centered in the South), which resembled a general strike in some respects. There was the famous 1968 sanitation workers strike in Memphis, where Dr. King was murdered. But there are also countless strikes that most of us have never heard of. In addition, there are actions that might not seem to fit the definition of a strike but very much are, such as what W. E. B. Du Bois described as the "great general strike" when African American slaves put down their tools en masse and left plantations following the Emancipation Proclamation.[3]

A strike is a form of direct power that workers possess. While every strike isn't victorious, it is an instrument that workers can directly use to make a point and attempt to address a grievance or injustice. There are also indirect forms of power that workers may possess, such as their support for certain political candidates or parties that they believe represent their interests.

During much of the history of capitalism, strikes have been illegal. They were often described as insurrectionary and, in fact, there were laws against strikes that were called variations on "anti-syndicalism acts."[4] It was believed and/or cynically portrayed that every strike was a form of anarcho-syndicalist radicalism. As a result, the government and/or corporations would regularly repress strikes, often quite violently. The infamous Ludlow Massacre in the early twentieth century was one such example,[5] but so, too, was the repression of striking textile and garment workers in 1934 in South Carolina, North Carolina, and Tennessee, in which strikers and their families were put into internment camps.

The employer class and the elite media have tended to portray almost all strikes as the result of the unreasonable demands and actions of workers. In some cases, the workers are portrayed as having been misled by radicals (for example, communists, socialists, anarchists, radical religious types). In other cases, they're depicted as led by organized crime. And in still other cases, the workers are simply seen as greedy and uncaring (such as the Professional Air Traffic Controllers, or PATCO, which went on strike in 1981 and was destroyed by President Ronald Reagan).

Why do workers strike? Well, the simplest answer is that a strike is one way workers can pressure an employer in the context of actual or de facto bargaining. This contrasts with the power that employers possess. Think about it for a second. If an employer is engaged in any degree of negotiating with one or more workers, it can resort to any of the following:

1. Termination
2. Suspension

3. Character defamation (which, even if disproven, may be damaging)
4. Transfer
5. Lawsuits
6. Harassment
7. Degrade or alter working conditions, or, for that matter, actually move the work in some cases
8. Or the threat to use any of these

And with each of these, there's the question of money. In other words, these actions are backed by the power of money.

Now, workers have a much more limited arsenal. They can

1. Strike
2. Picket but not strike
3. Boycott . . . under certain circumstances[6]
4. Initiate lawsuits . . . if they have the money
5. Carry out slowdowns and sick-outs
6. Lobby
7. File a grievance (depending on the nature of the issue)
8. Or threaten to use one or more of these

A comparison reveals that the employer, first, has money and access to more resources. Second, they can take immediate action against an individual or a group of individuals and, in many cases, wait out any litigation. Workers, on the other hand, rarely have the financial resources of an employer. If they aren't financially prepared to conduct a long struggle with an employer, they can find themselves in trouble. This is what's called a *power imbalance*.

In the early days of capitalism and during the days of slavery, workers, lacking the legal right to strike, resorted to other methods to make their point understood. Sabotage and boycotts were employed by underground groups. At a point when workers (and certainly slave workers) lacked elemental democratic rights and were subject to long hours and brutal repression for alleged or real insubordination, they took the steps they felt they needed to take to gain relief, freedom, or some modicum of respect. As a result, the wealthy elites created narratives about the alleged devilish activities of different worker groups, whether slaves or free. These stories, myths, and fears continue to resonate.

Because of the power imbalance, even workers who are free from slavery and have some level of basic democratic rights find themselves between a rock and a hard place when it comes to engaging an employer. They can't hold the employer in captive meetings, transfer the employer to a different site, terminate the employer for bad behavior, or stop the employer from obtaining legal assistance from counsel. As a result, they have to resort to those nonviolent pressure tactics (like strikes) to convince the employer that they can't be taken for granted and must be respected.

Because strikes can be so effective, the employer class has tried to limit the ability of workers to utilize them. Laws have been created that, on the one hand, grant workers the right to strike, but on the other, find means that employers can use to obstruct their viability. One such method is called "permanent replacements."

In the United States, we often rely on euphemisms. Instead of saying, for instance, that workers can be *fired* for going on strikes, courts have permitted employers to *permanently replace* striking workers. This simply means that workers are brought in during a strike to take the jobs of those who have gone on strike. For most people these permanent replacements are known as "scabs." When the strike ends, these permanent replacements often keep the jobs gained during the strike. This sounds like a firing, right? Well there's a catch: the strikers are not technically fired, they just can't get their jobs back until their position opens up. The firing of striking workers has been accomplished through a sleight of hand. As a result, workers have had to become very careful about how, when, and where they go on strike.

What makes the supposed danger of strikes that the political Right yells about so ironic is that they've steadily declined. The US Bureau of Labor Statistics has been recording work stoppages since 1947. Unfortunately, they don't distinguish between strikes and lockouts, but we'll leave that aside for a moment. A major stoppage involves a thousand workers for BLS. Consider the following:

- The average number of strikes in the last ten years has been 21 per year.[7]
- The average number of strikes in the 1950s was 352 per year.
- In 1952, there were 470 major work stoppages.[8]
- In 2009, there were 5 major stoppages.[9]

So, in effect, as the number of strikes has decreased, the anti-unionists have increased the rhetoric regarding the danger of unions and strikes.

For some people this fact may be a source of comfort. After all, a strike represents a disruption or inconvenience; fewer strikes, fewer sources of inconvenience. But fewer strikes can be—and, in fact, in the United States are—an indicator of eroding democracy. Strikes haven't been declining because of rising contentment among workers but rather due to various forms of repression that workers face when they do strike. Additionally, unions have encountered new tactical problems when striking due to changes taking place in the economic sphere.

Let's clarify these points. First and foremost, particularly since the introduction of the Taft-Hartley amendments to the National Labor Relations Act, striking has become more difficult and risky for unions. As mentioned earlier, various approaches that workers had been able to use to demonstrate power, such as workplace occupations and certain types of boycotts, were rendered illegal. But so, too, were certain approaches to strikes, such as what was once called *mass picketing*, or large numbers of striking workers surrounding a place of work or an entrance to a place of work. This is obviously a smart tactic because it discourages an employer from trying to bring in scabs, thereby leveling the playing field. This went out the window when employers obtained the right to gain a court injunction against mass picketing, thereby limiting the number of workers who could be on a picket line. With such a limitation, a picket line became a symbolic action rather than a demonstration of strength.

Permanent replacements or the de facto firing of striking workers was, of course, an additional factor that swung the balance of power solidly toward the employer in a contractual battle.

The problem was, however, not just a matter of repression. The world of work changed, and many unions didn't keep up and consider the tactical implications. In some cases, the situation was very dramatic, such as in the textile and garment industries where employers could relatively easily shut down production and move. More dramatic changes in the world of work, such as the *internationalization of production* in many industries, affected striking. What this references is that industries, such as auto, developed the ability to produce the same product in different countries, so that if one workplace shut down another could take up the slack. This change in the world of work was not accidental but sought to weaken the power of workers in any one particular workplace.

There were and are today, of course, other reasons which account for the decline of strikes, including the unease on the part of many so-called mainstream union leaders to upset status quo and be perceived as being disruptive and troublemakers, and many workers questioning whether the tactic represents sufficient power to win their demands.

The decline has meant that workers have a decreasing ability to bargain successfully at the negotiating table. The illegalization of various nonviolent pressure tactics has meant that the employer class has more of the cards, so to speak, and can set the terms. In effect, workers are asked to throw themselves into a shark tank and swim while their hands are tied and they are blindfolded. While the employer class, as a whole, doesn't care about fairness, they should because the elimination of nonviolent pressure tactics can and frequently does lead to tactics of desperation. The desperation can be anything from a high turnover of the workforce, to other acts of desperation by organized workers who believe they have no choice if they want to get the attention of the employer and gain their respect.

47

MYTH 6

"UNIONS WERE GOOD ONCE, BUT WE DON'T NEED THEM ANY LONGER."

I had a discussion with a certain rich capitalist some years ago in what was supposed to be a social setting. After exchanging pleasantries, he offered his commentary on my chosen mission in life: the rebuilding of a viable labor movement. Unaware that he was regurgitating a familiar myth, he stated, "Unions were important once, but we don't need them any longer—they've gotten in the way. We've addressed the reasons that brought unions into existence."

Well, not so fast, Mr. Rich Man. History and reality aren't quite that simple.

When someone claims that unions were good once, what they're saying is that the days of crude industrialization, horrid working conditions, and miserable pay are over. There's a grudging acknowledgment from the Right that unions were responsible for the advancements that took place.

Interestingly, this argument was far more common in the 1970s and 1980s, but recently, as neoliberal thought has become more prominent, some question whether unions were *ever* of any value. But we will leave that aside for now.

There are multiple histories of the origins of trade unionism; the late Philip S. Foner, for instance, produced a multivolume classical work on the labor movement, and countless other noted labor historians produced important works.

Unions played a critical role in reshaping the lives of US workers because they constituted a movement for economic justice. At their height in the 1930s and 1940s, they energized other social movements and played a major role in pressing for progressive social and economic legislation. While great advances in progressive legislation had started earlier in the twentieth century, the union movement made the fight for progress and economic justice a mass cause, such as fighting against child labor and for codifying the eight-hour day. Unions pressured President Franklin Roosevelt and congressional Democrats to pursue the New Deal reforms, and after World War II, many unions believed in Roosevelt's hope for an Economic Bill of Rights. Though no such Economic Bill of Rights ever became law, the significant size of the union movement had an impact on working conditions, benefits, and wages/salaries not only in the unionized sector of the economy, but in the non-union sector as well. At its best, labor unionism was a mass cause supported not only by union members but also by people who weren't members or might never end up in labor unions.

SO, WHAT HAS CHANGED?

From the 1930s through the early 1970s, various mass movements—including but not limited to the labor movement—secured many social, economic, and political protections through the introduction of laws and regulations. In the case of labor unions, many of the victories won through collective bargaining were codified in contracts that most people never thought would or could be reversed. This included full pensions, relative job security, and pay raises with increases in productivity, not to mention overtime pay after thirty-five or forty hours. This was true not only in the United States, but also in much of the advanced capitalist world.

By the early 1970s, however, another tendency emerged as "stagflation" (economic stagnation plus inflation) gripped the country, and public support for unions began to change in ways that continue to adversely affect workers.

Competition from more vital economies had a critical impact

on the United States, which had been the dominant capitalist economy since World War II. By the 1970s, however, it had lost much of its dynamism as new technologies that outmatched America's older technologies emerged in the Federal Republic of Germany, Japan, and Sweden.

Greater demands were put on government and the employer class by workers (and various social movements) who sought to improve their standard of living and take advantage of increases in productivity. In fact, during the mid-to-late 1960s, it was a common assumption that with technological advances and productivity increases the workweek could be significantly cut over the following decades producing a situation where leisure time would expand as the workweek contracted. This was a rational assumption that didn't take into account the greed of the employer class.

New technologies that were either developed in the United States or imported had an impact on the work process, making it easier for companies to shift work to other parts of the United States or offshore. Additionally, and quite ironically, tax incentives were used to encourage US businesses to create jobs overseas, in part due to the Cold War fight with communism.

The 1970s weren't a gateway decade into a new, less stressful, and less time-intensive world of work. Instead, it was almost as if someone threw a car into reverse without first braking, and the screeching and clanging of gears reverberated throughout society. Naomi Klein in her must-read *The Shock Doctrine*[1] illuminates the dynamics within capitalism in this period in the 1970s and the choices that were undertaken. In brief, there were significant debates within the employer class, both in the United States and elsewhere, about which road to travel. What came together by the end of the decade and certainly by the early 1980s was an economic approach that was eventually known as "neoliberalism."[2]

A prototypical form of neoliberalism was constructed in Chile in the aftermath of the CIA-backed coup against the democratically elected socialist president Salvador Allende. A variant of neoliberalism was implemented in New York City in 1975 during the city's fiscal crisis. By the early 1980s, neoliberalism was widely known through its articulation by British prime minister Margaret Thatcher and President Ronald Reagan. Neoliberalism was an economic approach that suggested that the entire framework constructed under the New Deal was wrong. It was based on the powerful myth that the so-called free market was the solution to every economic problem. Government "interference," as neoliberals called it, threw the free market off-kilter.

At its core, neoliberalism believes in the removal of all obstacles to the accumulation of maximum profits. Therefore, adherents to neoliberalism promote deregulation (including environmental deregulation), casualization,[3] privatization, free trade, the elimination of labor unions and other worker organizations, and the elimination of the concept of the common or public good. In each case, neoliberalism argues that it seeks to remove unnecessary, wasteful, unproductive obstacles to economic vitality. In Klein's analysis, a variation of this could first be implemented after the Chilean coup due to the absence of any level of popular resistance (which was militarily suppressed).

In the midst of the 1970s upheaval and the emergence of neoliberalism, a little-noticed change was underway: the living standard of the average US working person was beginning to drop. Since the 1970s, this decline hasn't abated.

Under different presidential administrations that embraced varying forms of neoliberalism, decent living conditions gradually began to disappear. It didn't take place all at once and, at least in the initial stages, didn't seem to be necessarily permanent. However, as each layer was removed, working people came to accept this decline as inevitable.

Not surprisingly, there is a correlation between the decline of the living standard of workers and the decline of unions. In July 2011, the *American Sociological Review* published a study on the relationship between union decline and wage inequality that concluded, "In the early 1970s, unions were important for delivering middle class incomes to working class families, and they enlivened politics by speaking out against inequality . . . These days, there aren't big institutional actors who are making the case for greater economic equality in America."[4]

In other words, the living standard that had been attained by the mid-1970s wasn't simply the result of the economic productivity of US capitalism or its relationship to the rest of the world (though these were significant factors), but rather, it was achieved in part through the struggles of working people through their labor unions.

Therefore, labor unions were not only critical in the eradication of the horrendous conditions of the early twentieth century, but their *absence* was directly linked to the decline in living standards and the reemergence of forms of economic conditions that many people had believed to be extinct.

In considering the question of continued relevance of unions, it's useful to examine economic conditions generally as well as the actual conditions of work. One way to look at this is through the re-newed growth of sweatshops along with the evolution of the retail industry. But, first, let's consider a few points about the conditions of work that are often forgotten, ignored, or just taken for granted.

GIVING UP THE CONSTITUTION

In the late 1990s, the esteemed writer and activist Barbara Ehren-reich delivered a speech at the headquarters of the national AFL-CIO, the largest federation of labor unions in the United States. In her lecture, she offered a diplomatic critique of the labor union movement's approach toward organizing and recruiting workers. Her critique was unusual, however, because it focused on some-thing that labor union organizers often take for granted in their discussions with workers about why to organize or join a union: the absence of civil liberties in the non-union workplace.[5]

What struck me in listening to her was her discussion of the workplace. She pointed out what should be obvious: when workers enter into a non-union workplace, they surrender their Constitu-tional rights. Or, to put it in another way that has become increas-ingly popular, corporations have more rights than people!

This may seem a bit jarring, but that's only because we separate our lives and reality from what we've come to expect in a workplace and what we actually experience. First, keep in mind we're discussing most workplaces in the United States, the majority of which lack a legitimate labor union. So, think about the world of the workplace this way:

- There is no freedom of speech: if you speak out of turn, you can be punished and even terminated. Likewise, if you advocate forming a labor union, you can be terminated, even though it is illegal (but most employers know that the penalties for such terminations are minimal).
- There is no freedom of the press: if you issue your own publication, such as a flyer, you can be punished.
- There is no freedom of association: unless you can prove to the NLRB that you are engaged in your statutory right to self-organization, you can be charged with insubordination and punished by your employer.
- There is no freedom of movement: if you are not in close proximity to your work area—and, in some cases, if you are not at your work station—you can be punished.
- You can be searched at any time when on the premises of work.
- You are guilty until proven innocent: an employer can terminate you for any reason or no reason as long as you cannot demonstrate that such termination was due to a violation of your statutory rights, e.g., against unlawful discrimination, a violation of the NLRA.

Most of us don't reflect on the fact that in the absence of either special legislation or organization in the workplace, so-called property rights trump your personal civil liberties.

And because most of us don't consciously think about this reality, we assume that if and when we're terminated or face a workplace injustice, there's a law to protect us. Usually there isn't. I personally came up against this when I worked as an employment paralegal in Boston in the 1980s. Three workers who had been employed by an airline shipping company were suddenly fired for no apparent reason, though the workers had heard rumors about allegations against them. They came into the office where I worked to describe what happened, and I was certain they had been victimized by their employer. Unfortunately, there was no law to protect them: their statutory rights had not been violated; they had not been fired in order for the employer to benefit monetarily by receiving something these employees were supposed to receive (for example, a commission of some sort); and they had not been engaged in any form of self-organization. They had simply been the victims of a faceless workplace injustice, and there was no law to protect them, including no law that would insist an employer explain the firing at all.

The nonexistence of workplace rights that we would take for granted on the street demonstrates that unions are just as relevant as they ever were. Particularly since there is no indication that Congress or most state legislatures will be taking steps to increase protection for workers—at least soon—workers either have to rely on luck, or they have to take steps through self-organization to guarantee that their rights and their voices are respected.

THE PAST IS NEVER REALLY THE PAST . . .

The victory of progressive legislation in the mid-twentieth century, along with the rise of labor unions, led many to believe we were approaching a more humane workplace. The lack of Constitutional rights in the workplace should disabuse everyone of that, but what has been more startling has been the return to workplace conditions reminiscent of the early twentieth century.

Changes in capitalism have affected both the production processes and the structure of employment. To put this another way, once upon a time, certainly for most of the twentieth century, an individual worked for a company or governmental body and understood that he or she existed as an employee of that given organization. With the growth of neoliberalism, however, that began to change. Contracting out of work, or subcontracting, has risen to become a major feature of work-life.

No doubt you're probably familiar with how this works. Companies and governmental bodies choose to focus on what they call their "core functions" and anything outside of the core is subject to being subcontracted. When it's subcontracted, the main employer is no longer concerned with legal obligations toward those workers. They simply deal with the contractor. If they decide they don't like the work of the contractor, they get rid of them, usually with thirty days' notice.

In the rush to cut costs, those costs associated with workers are always on the chopping block. Using contractors to handle workers becomes an easy matter for the main company. If there is unrest at the contractor's firm, the main company gets rid of the contractor. Additionally, the main company can hide behind the contractor and claim ignorance when issues arise regarding the behavior of the contractor.

As a result of these changes, we've witnessed the reemergence of sweatshops right here at home. There are many and varied examples. According to the National Mobilization Against Sweatshops, in 1995, seventy-two Thai slaves were found working twenty-two hours a day under threats of physical violence inside a barbed-wire facility in El Monte, California.[6] Sweatshops are not always as crude. As writer and activist Jennifer Gordon noted:

> Like their predecessors, some of today's sweatshops can be found in the New York or Los Angeles garment industry. But with American garment production evaporating even as I write, new kinds of sweatshops—with the same long hours, low wages and high rates of injury—are emerging. They have followed jobs from manufacturing to service, and new immigrants from cities to suburbs. Sweatshops now flourish in restaurants . . . which pay far less than the minimum wage; in landscaping,

where workers mow 50 or more lawns in a day; in car washes and construction; in home renovation and auto repair; in domestic work.[7]

What was thought of as a thing of the past has returned with a vengeance, albeit with a slightly different facade. In fact, sweatshops have entered the high-tech world. Through the importation of labor from places such as South Asia, the high-tech and financial segments of the economy have engaged in newer forms of sweatshops. In an important 2009 expose, *Bloomberg Businessweek* noted:

Tech service outfits . . . have thrived in recent years because of shifts in the U.S. economy. As cost-cutting pressures have increased, companies turned over management of tech systems and other back-office operations to outsourcing firms, including many that bring workers from India and other countries into the U.S. on temporary visas such as H-1B.

One important way outsourcers hold down costs is by keeping a lean workforce at each client site—then turning to smaller companies . . . when they need to increase staff for specific projects, such as installing new software or building a new Web site. These companies are known as "body shops" because of their role, and often rely heavily on foreign workers who come into the country on H-1Bs and other visas. . . . A study by the federal government last year estimated that 54% of visa rule violations were committed by companies with fewer than 25 employees.[8]

The story details the creation of indentured servant–like conditions for the workers who are imported, many under false pretenses. They're often underpaid through misrepresenting the actual location of work to avoid federal wage standards. And hiding behind these small contractors are larger employers that can distance themselves from the actual practices of the contractors, while taking advantage of the terms under which these contractors employ labor.[9]

As Jennifer Gordon noted, in the original wave of sweatshops, legal standards were only part of the equation in overcoming them; labor unions were the other. The famous International Ladies' Garment Workers' Union, a key union in organizing a largely female workforce in the sweatshops of the early twentieth century, was a key factor in weakening sweatshops in the early to mid-twentieth century, but the change in the production process has made it both more likely that sweatshops could be reborn, and also more difficult for unions to organize.[10] Nevertheless, the labor union is the missing piece in ending sweatshops, and their relative absence from the scene, along with weakened governmental enforcement, has meant that it is a case of déjà vu or, as baseball icon Yogi Berra once said, "Déjà vu all over again."

One effort that has sought to address the changes in working conditions brought on by neoliberalism has been the Justice for Janitors campaign of the Service Employees International Union. Though not organizing sweatshop workers, it is noteworthy as a campaign that developed in direct response to a change in the way the janitorial industry operated. With the growth of janitorial contractors, SEIU could not organize each contractor one at a time and expect to win unless they found a way to put pressure on the building owners and turn the entire matter into a public issue. With this approach, SEIU won some stunning victories.

Activists examining the terrain of so-called postindustrial United States have been thinking about new approaches to organizing given the restructuring that has taken place in so many industries and the reemergence of sweatshops. Without a doubt, labor unions are not a thing for yesterday; they are every bit as relevant to the conditions facing workers today.

MYTH 7

"UNIONS ARE ONLY NEEDED BY WORKERS WHO HAVE PROBLEMS AND GET INTO TROUBLE."

When I first began my career as a union organizer, I would hear similar objections from workers I approached to form a labor union in their workplace. One of the most common went like this: "Labor unions are only needed by workers who have problems or get into trouble. I do my job and don't get into trouble, so a union is irrelevant to me." For many union organizers, this response was perplexing.

Implicit in this statement are two dangerous assumptions. First, it's fairly easy to stay out of "trouble" at work if you do the right thing and keep your nose clean, so to speak. And second, it reveals a commonly held narrow view of the union's role.

Let's start with the question of "trouble." This broad characterization is ultimately about power and authority, specifically, who has the power and authority and who doesn't. But in a workplace, not only are nonorganized workers powerless, but also "trouble" can arise from any number of sources. It can be based on having been trained for a position and not performing it competently, having a bad attitude, and certainly on criminal or semi-criminal behavior.

Yet "trouble" can arise from other nebulous circumstances. It might be that a supervisor or manager simply has it out for you; it might arise out of some form of discrimination or favoritism, having to do with race, gender, ethnicity, sexual orientation, age, or religion.[1] It might emerge because of an ongoing conflict about how things operate in the workplace. Or it might originate due to some arbitrary decision(s) made by a supervisor.

For this reason, it's important that we not accept the notion of "trouble" at face value but delve deeper. To be clear, a labor union is a very useful device for workers who have any range of difficulties in the workplace. At the least, a labor union functions like an insurance program; it may be something that you never utilize, but it's there just in case. For those who think that they'll never get into trouble, they have to ask themselves a few questions:

- What happens if there is a new supervisor who doesn't care for me?
- What happens if the company is bought by someone else?
- If I'm in the public sector, what happens if a new administration is elected?
- What happens as I get older and can't perform my job the same way I did when I was twenty-five?
- What happens if I'm injured on the job?
- What happens if a new technology is introduced?
- What happens if my shift is changed and my salary plummets?

Get the picture? Things change—life is unpredictable. To assume that you're safe and sound is as naive as assuming that because you're a good driver you'll never get in a car accident.

If for no other reason than providing a modicum of security, it's comforting to know there are mechanisms to challenge unfair, unilateral, or biased actions. This doesn't guarantee you'll win, but it does provide for the possibility.

Yet, there is something else contained in the notion that the union is only focused on those who have problems or are in trouble. It's actually a critique of a form of trade unionism that places significant resources on the needs of the numerical minority of members who file grievances.

Let's stop for a minute and explain something about the process that exists in most collective bargaining agreements/contracts to handle problems: the grievance procedure. Here's a summary of how this works:

1. An action is taken against a worker due to an alleged disciplinary infraction or, separately, the worker perceives there has been a violation of his/her rights as contained in the collective bargaining agreement.
2. With the help of his union shop steward,[2] the worker files a grievance or formal complaint with his/her immediate supervisor. The supervisor has a certain amount of time to respond.
3. If the worker disagrees with the response, he can appeal it to another level of management. The worker and his steward may have a meeting with this next level of management in hopes of resolving the problem.
4. If the worker's grievance is denied, at this point, there might be another level for purposes of appeal within the company or organization, or the grievance might be taken to arbitration. Arbitration is a process along the lines of a less formal court. A neutral individual—called an arbitrator—is hired by both the company/organization and the labor union to decide on matters the two sides cannot resolve. The arbitrator makes his or her decision based on the wording of the contract, prior decisions, and past practice. Both sides may make arguments, submit legal briefs, and call witnesses.
5. The arbitrator makes his or her decision after considering all the available evidence, the credibility of both sides, and the history of the issue.
6. In general, an arbitrator's decision cannot be appealed to a court of law. The decision is final.[3]

Due to the complexity of a *legitimate* grievance procedure, efforts can be exceedingly time consuming and very demanding of both the grievant as well as union officials and staff.[4] In addition, union staff and officials have to perfect litigation skills to be competent representatives. In effect, this means they're prevented from doing other union activities they might otherwise do.

But there's also another side to this problem. Ours is a litigious society, and we assume that, first, there must be a law guaranteeing a proper resolution of every problem, and second, if we get a competent representative—more often than not a lawyer—truth, justice, and the "American way" will assure our victory. The real world is a bit more complicated.

In this litigious society, many union members believe that to gain proper representation, they must rely on a lawyer and no one else. The second, and related problem, is that many union representatives believe that to be taken seriously they must act like lawyers, if not become them. As a result, there has been a tendency over the years for many union officials and staff to focus on becoming semi-lawyers and engaging in grievance confrontations rather than focusing on the larger mission of labor unions.

This focus on litigation has led some unions to place a premium on the hiring of attorneys, rather than staff capable of organizing, educating, and mobilizing members. Some labor union leaders believe that they prove their dedication and sincerity by providing members with attorneys or quasi-attorneys to handle disputes. Instead, this reinforces in the minds of many members that unions exist for those who face trouble rather than those who go to work, do their jobs, and go home at the end of their shift.

In sum, labor unions are important mechanisms for workers who face difficulties at work. Since difficulties are unpredictable, and happen to the best of us, it's better to have access to legitimate representation than to none at all. Yet this begs the question of whether this alone is enough of a reason for labor unions to exist.

ALTERNATIVES

> The essence of trade unionism is social uplift. The labor
> movement has been the haven for the dispossessed,
> the despised, the neglected, the downtrodden, the poor.
> —*A. Philip Randolph*

As I've suggested, there are different ideas about what it means
to be a trade unionist and what a labor union's core mission should
be. African American labor leader,[5] president of the Brotherhood
of Sleeping Car Porters, and a key player in the civil rights movement of the 1950s and '60s, A. Philip Randolph offered a remarkably different vision of trade unionism. For Randolph, the essence
of trade unionism wasn't handling grievances or arbitrating cases.
Instead, he framed the mission of the labor unions in terms of a
social movement, and actually a social movement for a wide breadth
of the population.

When unions break out of the confines of workplace litigation,
they engage in various activities that go beyond focusing exclusively
on workers who are in trouble, such as ensuring workers have a
voice at work. In fact, this is something John Sweeney emphasized
when he was elected president of the AFL-CIO in 1995 and began a
series of organizational reforms. One goal was to expand the view
of organizing and recruiting workers. Giving workers a voice in
the workplace actually speaks to resisting the authoritarian atmosphere of most work environments, something that workers take
for granted, but don't particularly enjoy.

Unions, when thinking outside of the proverbial box, can also
become genuine instruments for justice. Here are a few examples:

- One of my favorite stories concerns the United Packinghouse
  Workers of America (now part of the United Food and Commercial Workers Union), which in the 1940s and 1950s fought
  against racially discriminatory hiring policies. What made this
  so unique is that most unions believed they could and should
  do nothing about employment injustices until a worker was

formally hired. The Packinghouse Workers chose to push the envelope.

- In the immediate aftermath of World War II, the Congress of Industrial Organizations raised the demand for national health insurance, a reform to cover everyone and not just workers who were fortunate enough to win this in their collective bargaining agreements.

- In more recent times, local unions affiliated with the Service Employees International Union and, separately, with the California Nurses Association/National Nurses United—to name just these two—have taken up struggles around patient/nurse ratios to guarantee that patients receive the best care and nurses are not overwhelmed.

- Unions have addressed matters of new technology in the workplace. This can range from ergonomic issues to design. When I worked for the National Postal Mail Handlers Union, for instance, we negotiated a provision with the US Postal Service for union involvement at the conceptual stage when new technology was being considered. The union known as the Bakery, Confectionery, Tobacco Workers and Grain Millers International Union has also been actively involved in workplace technology issues.

- The American Federation of Government Employees has been negotiating "telework" provisions such that individual workers can conduct significant amounts of their work from home-based or distanced locations rather than commuting each day (assuming that their job lends itself to such a provision).

The list could go on. The point is that many unions have sought not only to negotiate agreements that affect a broad spectrum of the membership or bargaining unit, but—in the spirit of Randolph's vision—they've also sought to expand collective bargaining to a broader definition of economic justice.

An interesting example of combining the fight for one's own members and making a broader social statement occurred in the late 1980s and early 1990s when Local 26 of the Hotel and Restaurant Employees (now UNITE HERE) in Boston engaged in a major struggle with key hotels in the city. During the 1980s, Local 26 had become well known as a fighting union that mobilized its members at contract time and reached out to the broader community for support. They were an exciting and pathbreaking union.

One of the issues they encountered, within their membership, was the fact that it was becoming far too expensive to live in Boston. The cost of housing, whether apartments or homes, was skyrocketing, and workers were being chased out of the city, forced in many cases to live in more distant suburban towns (some of which were known as "dead cities"). The leadership, under then-president Dominic Bozzotto, made the issue of affordable housing the central issue for the campaign. They made a demand for the creation of a housing trust fund such that the members of Local 26 would have access to funds to afford a security deposit on an apartment or a down payment on a home. They not only won this demand, which necessitated some changes in the law by the way, but this effort took off, ultimately resulting in the creation of a union-affiliated (and now independent) organization known as the Neighborhood Assistance Corporation of America that fights predatory lenders and helps gain housing for lower income people.

What's important to remember is that while the claim that unions only focus on those in trouble is partially true, at the same time it misses labor's amazing potential to broaden the fight for economic justice. Too many labor leaders fear that to turn away from traditional labor unionism (and especially workplace litigation) will lead to a membership backlash and charges that the union is abandoning its core mission. Instead, it would be useful for these same leaders to consider that a broader vision of trade unionism might bring forward an entirely new and energized segment of the membership that had previously felt disengaged.

"THE UNION USES OUR MONEY FOR POLITICAL ACTION AND I HAVE NO SAY IN THE MATTER!"

It should now be apparent there are many different ways to approach the question of unions and political action. Likewise, there are plenty of legal issues at stake when it comes to unions in political and legislative matters. When most people raise questions about unions and politics, they aren't talking about the law; they're talking about how one interprets the mission of unions and what they see—rightly or wrongly—as the relative power of labor unions.

WHY DO LABOR UNIONS GET INVOLVED IN POLITICAL AND LEGISLATIVE ACTION?

It's not uncommon for certain commentators to make a statement like: "Unions should just stay out of politics and focus on what's happening in the workplace!" Such statements almost sound neutral and unbiased, but they decidedly aren't. In fact, they ignore the realities faced by workers, not just in today's workplaces, but historically.

For public sector workers, their engagement in political and legislative action has a more obvious consequence. But this isn't true of the private sector.

Think about it for a moment. Does any workplace exist in isolation from the political and legislative worlds? Does the choice of this or that candidate for political office mean nothing? Consider this:

- Workplaces are affected by zoning ordinances.
- Workplaces are affected by taxes.
- Workplaces are affected by the existence or lack of health, safety, and illegal discrimination statutes.
- Workplaces are affected by public investment in infrastructure or by the failure to make such investments.
- Workplaces are affected by whether workers have the right to organize unions.
- Workplaces are affected by the level of unemployment and whether the unemployed have unemployment insurance.
- Workplaces are affected by trade legislation.

The list could easily continue. The fact is that workplaces don't exist in isolation, and the political and legislative decisions made each day have a direct impact on the work environment. Workers realized this basic truth a long time ago, but in the early years of the labor movement (broadly defined), those without property lacked the franchise (the ability to vote) so their involvement in the political arena was either indirect or tended to be more violent in response to injustice.

As workers began to form labor unions in the early to mid-nineteenth century, they also began to form political parties that represented the interests of working people, or more accurately, represented the interests of at least a segment of working people. The first labor parties, in fact, were formed in the United States. These early labor parties were a mixed bag of competing politics and programs (not to mention they generally ignored—and sometime outright excluded—women and people of color), but what they uniformly acknowledged was the fact that the demands of working people—at that point, largely free white men—necessitated politics and couldn't be resolved solely in workplaces.

For reasons having to do with both the nature of the US electoral system (the winner-take-all system that makes it difficult for "third parties" to electorally succeed above the local level) plus decisions that were made by the founders of the American Federation of Labor (in the early 1880s), independent labor parties became rarer. The AFL adopted the view that labor should explicitly not form its own parties but should, instead, lobby the existing parties, in this case the Democratic and Republican parties. That these parties were heavily dominated by the influence of wealth and corporations meant little to the AFL. The dominant view in the AFL held that the formation and existence of labor parties was both a practical problem as well as a political liability in that their existence implied a struggle between classes (workers and their allies versus the rich employers), which the AFL preferred to deny. Therefore, contrary to labor movements in much of the rest of the world, the AFL stood back from *independent working class political action*.

Thus, the involvement of unions in the political and legislative arenas isn't something new, but rather has been a component of trade unionism from the beginning. Even in labor movements that opposed established electoral politics, such as the Industrial Workers of the World (the IWW, known as the "Wobblies"), the union's activities were never restricted to the workplace. The IWW, inspired by anarcho-syndicalist politics, became legendary for the "free speech fights" of the early twentieth century. These fights were precisely about the right to speak freely without fear of government or corporate repression. Although these struggles were mass actions, their aim was to force government to rescind ordinances that restricted the right of union activists to speak openly. Leaving aside the IWW's vision of a *revolutionary* transformation through the overthrow of capitalism, it's important to note they remained a movement that saw the importance of mass involvement against large-scale repression.

WHAT IF UNIONS DID NOT ENGAGE IN POLITICAL AND LEGISLATIVE WORK?

Imagine you work for a company that produces automobiles, and because there are no "health and safety" statutes, many of your co-workers are becoming ill from something in the work environment. But there's no one to appeal to. To complicate the situation, imagine that the company's owner has obtained a special tax break from the city and doesn't have to pay taxes for the next five years. The owner is able to hire foreign workers who are unable to join your union and don't have the same rights as other workers. In fact, if they leave this employer, they'll be deported.

Now, assuming there's a union at this workplace, ask yourself whether these challenges are something they can handle by simply pressuring management. Perhaps some of them are, but if the company is a multinational conglomerate or is otherwise very strong, your ability to negotiate acceptable arrangements may be severely limited. In this situation, the labor union has no choice but to engage in political and legislative work to challenge the employer class who is advancing their own interests through legislative acts.

The employer class tends to turn to the political and legislative arenas to:

- Restrict the right of workers to organize and join unions.
- Seek special tax advantages to encourage them to invest or remain in the area, even if they do not need it. Consider, for instance, sports stadiums and the manner in which the owners of major teams turn to government for funding or financial inducements to remain in that city or to have a new stadium built.
- Oppose tax increases on the wealthy.
- Create employer-friendly regulations of all kinds.

Look closely and you'll see an interesting pattern emerging: the employers aren't necessarily looking out for the interests of one or two workplaces, but rather, for the interests of the employer class as a whole. One way they accomplish this is by forming organizations to advance their interests. These "trade associations" (and groups such as the Chamber of Commerce) represent the interests of employers in specific industries (or components of certain industries) and engage in an immense amount of political and legislative work.[1] With the advent of the notorious *Citizens United* Supreme Court decision (2010), corporations are able to pour vast sums of money into elections with little to stop them.[2] Yet ironically, it's these same employer groups and their front organizations that accuse the labor unions of inappropriately involving themselves in political and legislative work.

While labor unions will often engage in political and legislative work that goes beyond an individual workplace or an individual industry, they do so because it is frequently the case that the interests at stake affect workers as a whole. Protecting unemployment insurance, for instance, is not limited to a particular industry or workplace. And if a labor union were to say, hypothetically, that the issue of unemployment insurance does not directly affect their members, what happens if there is a major layoff or workplace closing? A labor union cannot afford to wait until their members are directly affected by a calamity before they address it at the broader political or legislative level.

The idea that labor unions shouldn't engage in political and legislative work flies against history and against the practice of the employer class. The day an employer renounces political and legislative involvement is the day one could imagine a labor union doing the same. But, really, don't hold your breath. The natures of class, politics, and power in our economic system drive all players into the political and legislative arena irrespective of their ideology and intent.

INTERNAL DISAGREEMENTS AND POLITICAL DECISIONS

If you accept that labor unions logically engage in political and legislative work to advance workers' interests, there remains the debate about *how* they engage.

In the 1800s, there was a proliferation of labor parties in the United States. This phenomenon declined toward the end of the century, when organized labor largely turned toward various forms of lobbying. Special committees within the labor union called political action committees or committees on political education were established and were responsible for identifying potential candidates to support in elections. Because of election-law restrictions, unions could financially support candidates only through special funds collected on a voluntary basis from members. In other words, if members did not want their money spent on candidates, they could easily refuse.

As labor unions grew in strength in the mid-twentieth century, fewer members participated in political and legislative campaigns, even if they financially contributed. This was the result of several factors, not the least being the impact of the Cold War. Whereas during the 1930s and early 1940s political action was widely exalted as part of the broader popular front against fascism, the Cold War paranoia in the 1940s weakened political engagement and resulted in a massive purge of leftists from unions.[3] In fact, inspired by the Cold War, dissent within many unions became suspect, and accusing someone of being a communist was a popular way to suppress opposition or silence non-mainstream opinions.

In this period, debate over political issues and candidates became more constricted and in some cases disappeared altogether. Political options within the union movement narrowed, as did the people who made the decisions. Thus, endorsements of candidates for political office tended to be made by executive boards, and there were rarely open debates about the relative merits of various candidates. It was almost unheard of for a union to have an internal binding poll regarding what stand it should take on various issues. This doesn't mean that all decisions were or are made by one or two people. Rather, decisions are largely the result of informal channels of communication and discussion capped off by a formal vote by the leading body of the particular union (for instance, the executive board of a local union or the national executive board of a national union). If you aren't part of that informal group, you have little say in the actual decision-making process—unless you have organized to make your opinion known.

This approach to decision making tended to alienate the rank-and-file members from the process who increasingly felt that their voices weren't heard. Smelling blood, right-wing pundits took advantage of a very real problem to focus on the question of involvement of labor unions in politics rather than on reforming decision-making processes. The approach of the political right, in either case, has been completely cynical since they almost never criticize corporations or wealthy conservatives for their involvement in political and legislative action.

Certainly, there are unions that engage in a more participatory process of decision making, but decision making alone is not the issue. As evidenced by the AFL-CIO's Common Sense Economics experiment, education is just as important. Commissioned in 1996 by the AFL-CIO's executive council, Common Sense Economics was a program aimed at raising the economic awareness of the membership of unions and creating a framework for their understanding of some of the basic issues of the economy and its impact on workers. There were several unique features of this program, most notably its interactive nature, which drew on the participants' existing knowledge but also challenged them to rethink their frameworks for understanding the economy. This was an exercise aimed at raising consciousness about class and power.

Educational programs like Common Sense Economics have been unique in the post–late 1940s purges of organized labor. For years, even a discussion of "class" was, for all intents and purposes, forbidden for fear of pro-communist allegations. In the post–Cold War world, the Red Scare has abated, but internal education about the economic big picture remains rare. Yet it is precisely this large-scale education that's paramount for achieving real democratic engagement by union members in the political and legislative arenas. If engagement in those arenas is to extend beyond the core leadership, then the membership must understand the stakes involved in political and legislative engagement. This can only be achieved through a dialogue with the members, by engaging them and introducing new information.

My own experience has revealed that when members are actually engaged in a discussion and their views are respected, the outcome can become one of inspired activism rather than cynical defeatism. This is the real meaning of the overused term "empowered."

"UNIONS HOLD ME BACK FROM ADVANCING, AND IF I JOIN I WILL NEVER BE PROMOTED."

One of the central arguments employers make to discourage workers from joining or forming labor unions is that unions are an obstacle to individual advancement. This is actually a variation on the theme addressed earlier: that unions allegedly spend their resources on workers who have problems or are in trouble, and that those who wish to excel are inhibited by unionization. The dark side of this, of course, is the implied retaliation from an employer if the worker proceeds to join a union or become active in one that has already been certified.

WHAT HAPPENS IN A WORKPLACE?

In a non-union workplace, the employer's largely arbitrary behavior reigns supreme. Ironically, the employer's unregulated, chance behavior may sometimes benefit a particular worker at a *specific* moment. Once I had a discussion with a worker from a non-unionized moving company. He said that few moving companies have unions, and that he had bounced around from one company to another seeking a good place to work. He then remarked that he's content at his current company because he had a "good boss." Our discussion ended there.

Most US workers depend on the personality and generosity of their bosses to survive and hopefully advance in the industry. But let's not forget what we've learned about the authoritarian world of work. As in any situation where only a few hold power, one's life largely depends on the whims of the elite clique that's running the show. If you're in the favor of the ruling faction, you can survive and sometimes thrive. If you're not, another fate awaits you.

While there may be personnel policies in place at a non-union company, the employer isn't legally obligated to respect them, a common source of misunderstanding among workers who are not in unions. There are no seniority provisions that an employer needs to respect, nor are there test standards that determine who receives a promotion. These decisions rest with the employer and the employer alone. The theory is that "merit" rules, but most workers know that this is simply not the case.

In such situations, the question comes down to who is more or less likely to gain from favoritism. Ask yourself, What are you prepared to do to obtain favoritism?

Let's return to the baseball analogy for a moment. Through most of its existence, Major League Baseball had something called the "reserve rule" or "reserve clause," which stipulated that a player was hired by a specific team and couldn't leave that team unless permitted to do so by the team's owner. The result was a modern version of indentured servitude. If you happened to be a good player on a successful team, you might be able to do well, at least by pre-1980 baseball standards. But if you were a good player on a not-so-good team, your career might be dead in the water.

All of this changed with the abolition of the reserve clause, the result of the combined work of Curt Flood, a very courageous St. Louis Cardinals outfielder, and the Major League Baseball Players Association, led by the brilliant strategist Marvin Miller. The struggle that the Players Association (the union of baseball players) conducted for an end to this system and the creation of "free agency" seemed to threaten the status of baseball's superstars, but what unfolded was something that surprised many people. The end to the reserve clause and the unilateral control of the future of the players by the owners resulted in tremendous opportunities for players across the teams. Rather than a very small number of superstars, baseball witnessed a rise in a broader array of players. A postscript is that this happened without a financial loss to Major League Baseball.[1]

So many workers are seduced by magical thinking, hoping against the odds they'll be able to work themselves into a position where they're in management's favor. Some take comfort in other people's success stories, but this is much like someone hitting the jackpot at a Las Vegas casino—the odds aren't in your favor.

MOVING FROM HOPE TO STRUCTURED FAIRNESS

A labor union seeks to win a collective-bargaining agreement or contract with an employer. The fundamental purpose of the collective bargaining agreement is to oppose favoritism and to set work and salary standards, not to impede the advancement of a worker. In other words, it's structured to guarantee fairness. For example, until the mid-1930s, hiring practices on the docks (in the longshore industry) were completely arbitrary. There was a system called the "shape up" that worked like a meat market[2] and was de facto corrupt. The general idea was that workers would gather at a particular location at a specific moment seeking work. A representative of one of the stevedore companies[3] would come out and pick the workers that the representative wanted. The company's representative could then demand kickbacks from the workers who were chosen. Further, they could ignore workers of color entirely and anyone who was considered a troublemaker (that is, a pro-union worker) would have little chance of being hired.

Beginning in 1934, dockworkers on the West Coast, in what came to be known as the International Longshore and Warehouse Union (ILWU), fought for a different, more equitable, hiring practice. Called the "hiring hall," this system regulated work placement by requiring laborers to register on a list, which then determined when and where they were dispatched. The West Coast dockworkers made sure that list was overseen by the union to ensure that bias or favoritism didn't enter into the picture. The 1934 General Strike in San Francisco won the hiring hall system, and the collective bargaining agreement codified it.

In establishing the hiring hall, the West Coast dockworkers weren't trying to halt the advance of any individual worker; exactly the opposite. They wanted to make sure that all workers had an opportunity, and, as such, they couldn't depend on chance or employer goodwill but rather on the creation of a system to ensure fairness.

BUT WHAT DO MANY EMPLOYERS SAY?

Here's where it gets interesting. I've experienced many times where an employer will say something like, "Hey, you know, I would love to give you more money . . . a promotion . . . but the union stops me. Sorry . . ."

What's critical to understand is that many employers will hide behind the collective bargaining agreement, or more accurately, the existence of the union, to justify not doing things they wouldn't otherwise do. This plays out in any number of ways in different industries. In the construction industry, you'll hear contractors claim their hands are tied with phrases like, "I'd hire you if it weren't for the union," when the reality is that they have no intention of hiring you in the first place.

Let's focus on a less dramatic example. Suppose there's a promotional opportunity at your company, and your collective bargaining agreement stipulates that the person with the greatest seniority gets the job. It might say something like, "After taking into account basic qualifications for the job, seniority will prevail." What does that mean?

Normally it means there are specific qualifications for the position and that you—the worker—need to be able to do X, Y, and Z proficiently. If you're unable to fulfill those requirements, seniority doesn't matter; you simply won't get the job.

I witnessed this firsthand when an administrative assistant

position opened up in a company where it was required that applicants type fifty words per minute. Someone could be put into that position on a temporary basis during which time they could take the typing test as many times as they wanted, but by the end of three months, they had to type fifty words per minute. If they weren't successful, seniority and personality were inconsequential—they wouldn't get the job.

Many employers like to say that seniority is the only factor, but it almost never is. More often than not, an employer simply doesn't want to evaluate the skills and performance of a worker. They opt instead for the easy route, and then blame the union for why someone who might have been "better" didn't get the job.

Is it fair to have a standard that includes seniority as a major factor in getting a job? Absolutely, and here's why. Person A might be an exceptional employee, but it's sometimes impossible to quantify such a subjective characteristic. If Person A and Person B can both do the job and neither has a mark against him or her (that is, disciplinary infractions), it stands to reason that the person with more experience should get the position. Person A might be exceptional, but his or her exceptional abilities don't *necessarily mean* he or she will do the job any better than Person B. Further, it's possible that Person A is actually "exceptional" because he or she has a more attractive personality, is more outgoing, or has other characteristics considered admirable but that generally have nothing to do with job performance.

Seniority also rewards dedication to an organization. Particularly at a time in history when people frequently change jobs, the fact that someone stays on board reveals a loyalty that needs to be acknowledged. But more importantly, there's frequent discrimination in the workplace, particularly against older workers and long-term workers. Employers often want to move in younger workers who they see as more flexible and often cheaper.

The point is that the existence of the labor union and the collective bargaining agreement don't prohibit advancement but, rather, provide a structure and framework to promote fair decisions.

Let's end this section by noting an experience that I've had on more than one occasion, and my guess is that you have as well. You started off on a job and, for a specific period, you had a great relationship with your boss. Then, perhaps suddenly, something happened. You might not have known what that "thing" was exactly, but your relationship has now clearly taken a dive; things aren't what they once were. Would you want your future to depend on such unpredictable circumstances or would you want to have criteria that depends less on someone's mood and attitude and more on something approaching objectivity?

"UNIONS ARE CORRUPT AND MOBBED UP!"

> Unions are very vulnerable to corruption . . . That's why they
> are attractive to organized crime in the first place, because it's so
> easy for the mafia to exploit the labor movement, but I think the
> McLaughlin case[1] is a good example of the magnitude of damage
> a corrupt individual can do to a union. He came from within, got
> control, and he looted it.[2]
>
> —*James Jacobs, director, New York University*
> *School of Law Center for Research in Crime and Justice*

One of the most difficult issues trade unionists frequently address
are accusations of corruption and mob (organized crime) influence
in the union movement. These allegations often come from individuals and groups that oppose trade unionism and are looking for
ways to undermine the right of workers to self-organize. But to deny
the existence of both corruption and organized crime does nothing
to raise the credibility of labor unions and labor unionism. In fact,
just the opposite occurs.

It's first important to distinguish between corruption and
the Mob, which to some may seem like a semantic distinction. As
James Jacobs suggested, these are distinct issues that need to be
understood.

Corruption exists in every institution, and unions aren't an exception. The type of corruption can take any number of forms, in-

cluding embezzlement, fraudulent elections, and bribery. Where money and power exists, corruption can emerge and spread like a disease.

Political pundits tend to condemn unions exclusively, but they're hardly the only institution that struggles with corruption. In May 2011, MSNBC ran a fascinating online series, "Some of America's Top Corporate Crooks," which included such notables as

- *Raj Rajaratnam.* Faces more than nineteen years in prison for using illegal tips in order to make trades through which he gained $60 million.
- *Bernie Madoff.* 150-year sentence for his notorious Ponzi schemes defrauding people of their life savings; approximately $6.9 billion in claims.
- *Ivan Boesky.* Jailed for insider training; built a $200-million fortune and paid $100 million in fines.[3]

What's striking in looking at the crimes of these few individuals is the staggering amounts of money involved. The Madoff scandal alone not only ruined countless lives and retirement possibilities, but it also destroyed institutions that trusted him with their investments.

Ironically, despite the extent of corporate corruption, with the exception of a small minority, many mainstream and right-wing pundits either tend to ignore such examples or they particularize it, focusing more on the psychological makeup of the perpetrators rather than any systemic problems. Yet when it comes to allegations or proven examples of corruption within the union movement, there's a different standard. The objectives are cynical, prompting many legitimate supporters of labor unions to dismiss all criticism at their own peril.

CORRUPTION

In general, a lack of financial control and regulation in any organization, including unions, makes corruption possible. What's striking in the case of labor unions is the all-too-common belief that the union leader is entitled to treat the organization's treasury as his or her personal bank. This can happen only when there is a lack of genuine democracy and/or a poor (or nonexistent) system of checks and balances. Corruption might be on a small scale, like using the union's credit cards to buy pizzas for one's family on a Friday evening, or it might be on a much larger scale, such as bribery, embezzlement, or the misuse of union funds in a political election. One situation that I am aware of started with a union official who received special benefits from a vendor. This official's expenses weren't scrutinized by the secretary-treasurer and were permitted without question. Trips, ostensibly on union business, were extended for personal use, and the union's credit card was abused. It's likely that any one of these activities wouldn't have resulted in the unraveling of the entire administration, but the accumulation of the incidents, accompanied by growing recklessness, led to the eventual exposure of the crimes.

In this instance, what permitted the corruption to go unnoticed was the extent to which others were drawn in, not as conspirators per se, but rather, as objective beneficiaries of the corruption. This is the trickle-down effect of corruption, which can undermine an entire organization. Individuals might be taken out to dinner or on a trip; they might be encouraged to charge certain personal expenses to their hotel room (paid by the union), or they might receive certain gifts. The form of corruption doesn't have to be big, but every misdeed undermines the integrity of those who might otherwise raise a flag of caution or danger regarding the situation.

Corruption can grow and spread through "termless" administrations. When leaders can run for office endlessly, they tend to create a protective coterie around them. Individuals in that coterie start to see their futures as being determined, to a great extent, by the future of that leading individual, rather than by the organization. As such, individuals in the coterie become highly protective of the leader, even if and when the leader acts irresponsibly and engages in questionable activities. To speak against the leadership might jeopardize the coterie members' careers, so they remain silent. In this case, corruption manifests itself in the simple act of denial or turning a blind eye to unethical and in some cases illegal behaviors and activities.

That said, unions are under tremendous levels of scrutiny by various governmental institutions, meaning that unlike corporations, which can move vast amounts of money to overseas accounts, unions have to be quite careful about their financial affairs. Government-required reports designed to root out corruption are foisted on unions often to the point of being burdensome. Thus, while corruption certainly exists in some unions, it's demonstrably not a phenomenon that afflicts the labor movement as a whole. There will always be examples of corrupt union officials who attempt to "game" the system, however. As I've repeatedly mentioned, an educated membership is a critical safeguard against these problems.

THE MOB

The history of organized crime, and the Mafia in particular, is often misunderstood when it comes to the union movement. While all Mob activity is evidence of corruption, not all corruption is evidence of Mob activity, yet the two are often conflated. Recall the instance of corruption previously mentioned about the local union official using the union's credit cards for personal expenses. This individual was corrupt, but in this particular local union, this wasn't evidence of Mob influence.

In the history of trade unionism, there have been several unions that, at various points, have been significantly penetrated by the Mob. These have included the Laborers International Union of North America, the Hotel Employees and Restaurant Employees International Union (now known as UNITE HERE), the International Brotherhood of Teamsters, and the International Longshoremen's Association (the dockworkers on the East Coast and Gulf Coast). Many other unions, including the Service Employees International Union, have struggled with Mob influence in years past. The four mentioned above, however, have been the subject of federal investigations at various times.

James Jacobs authored a major study of mobs and unions entitled *Mobsters, Unions, and Feds*.[4] Additionally, in the 1980s, the federal government, through the President's Commission on Organized Crime, conducted an investigation along with a series of hearings on the question of Mob influence in labor unions. The published report—issued during the Reagan presidency—continues to provide insight decades later.[5]

Understanding the legacy of the Mob in labor unions means stepping away from gross characterizations and looking very carefully at the nature of the problem. The report from the President's Commission on Organized Crime, much of which makes for quite interesting, if sobering, reading, offers the following qualifications that are worth noting when one hears the rants of anti-union folk:

> In naming these four international unions we are not saying
> that all of the locals of these unions are controlled or even
> influenced by organized crime. As testimony before the Commission will show, some very courageous local officers have
> on occasion and at great risk defied racketeer control. But of
> the approximately 50,000 labor organizations in the U.S. with
> a total of over $9 million in assets, the law enforcement analyses are that about three to four hundred locals are heavily influenced or controlled by organized crime syndicates. Many of
> these, however, are very major locals embracing thousands
> of members in strategic cities, enabling gangster domination
> of the internationals, even though in the majority of the locals
> the officers and the membership are not corrupt.[6]

This statement is quite significant. For one, the commission was focusing on the major sites of Mob influence and not making a broad-brush criticism. Second, the number of locals affected by Mob influence was an insignificant percentage of the labor organizations. While none of this may matter to a worker in a mobbed-up union, what's important for the reader to keep in mind is scale. To this should be added that major inroads against Mob influence have been made in the intervening years.

That said, it's worth exploring how and why the Mob penetrated unions. But we must be careful when we simply say it's about money—this doesn't mean that the Mob is only, or in some cases mainly, interested in stealing money from a local or national union. But rather there is access to various pots of money—the workers' money—they can get their hands on. They can also use their influence in a union to intimidate employers, or serve as a de facto mercenary army for an employer that wishes either to crush a militant wing of a particular union or to crush a rival, legitimate union. Control of pension funds and health and welfare funds is often a major goal of mobsters when penetrating unions. With such control, money can be siphoned off, contracts that condone Mob businesses can be instituted, and questionable investments can be made. Like a cancer, Mob influence can take the life out of an organization as resources are drained.

The 1985 report offers important insight into the history of Mob influence in unions. The following is a useful synopsis in understanding the phenomenon:

> Perhaps the most common feature of unions most severely
> influenced by racketeers is a membership comprised of
> unskilled or semi-skilled workers. . . . Corruption has also
> tended to appear among unions where the membership is
> transient, frequently due to the irregular schedule of work,
> (e.g., the early building trades union, I.L.A.); geographically
> scattered, due to the dispersion of job sites, (e.g., Teamsters,
> I.L.A., building trades); immigrant; or where the membership
> is made insecure by intense competition for jobs. The effect
> of these factors is a rank and file that is reluctant, if not unable,
> to organize against mob or corrupt domination. The epitome
> of susceptibility in this regard was the I.L.A. of the 30's and

40's; the mason tenders, or hod carriers, are probably the best current examples. For comparison's sake it is worthwhile to consider the United Auto Workers, with relatively few concentrated, stable work places, and a more established and confident membership.[7]

The point here is that certain unions have proven uniquely susceptible to Mob influence either because of the structure of the industry or the vulnerable nature of the workforce. Being able to organize against the Mob is particularly important because it suggests that in industries or sectors that have a transient workforce, there is, in effect, a lack of incentive on the part of a critical mass of workers to engage in anti-Mob organizing.

As with the problem of corruption, there are no easy solutions to eliminate Mob influence, but the report has two points worth noting. The first: "A vulnerable membership may nevertheless be protected by a tradition of idealism in the union leadership . . . a belief that unionism was 'a cause, not a business.'"[8] The second: "While not always an effective tool against labor racketeers, democratic processes at least contain the potential for change."[9]

The "tradition of idealism" is evocative and surprising considering this document hails from the Reagan era. Yet it's precisely the right orientation and recognizes that unionism is a cause that strives for equity and has led many men and women to make great sacrifices for their fellow workers. It's also led to intense struggles to ensure that the union stays true to its origins.

Nevertheless, such traditions can become frayed or alternatively ossified over time unless steps are taken to rejuvenate the organization. This is where member education combined with a culture of involvement and activism becomes crucial. For this reason, I return to the second suggestion, that matter of democracy. Democratic practices are fundamentally important, but they need to be linked with a culture of labor idealism for them to mean anything. Democratic practices without the inspiration of solidarity can become very mechanical and, ultimately, meaningless.

While there are certain types of unions and certain workforces that may be more susceptible to Mob influence, it can happen anywhere. Some unions, as the report also notes,[10] utilized the Mob in their early days to fight employers, just as employers had used the Mob to fight unions. In other cases, legitimate union leaders made arrangements with individuals they may not have realized were mobbed up. And, perhaps most dangerous of all, otherwise virtuous union members choose to deny Mob connections in the hope that they can simply work around them.

Thus, while the issue of the Mob isn't *the* major problem facing unions, it'd be wrong to act as if it weren't a problem. Reform movements in unions such as the Teamsters, the Laborers, and the ILA have challenged mobbed-up union officials and practices, sometimes naming it for what it is and other times, perhaps tactically, choosing to move against such opponents less directly.[11] In either case, the objective is the same: return the union to its members and out of the hands of corrupt individuals.

"UNIONS HAVE A CHECKERED HISTORY AND WERE STARTED BY COMMUNISTS AND OTHER TROUBLEMAKERS."

A familiar refrain since the rise of a labor movement is that labor unions are run by radicals and that they're disruptive. What should now be evident is that unions aren't in any formal sense ideological organizations, but rather, they're created by workers in response to particular economic conditions. As I noted, they aren't the only possible response, but they're one that workers have gravitated to in order to address their immediate (and in some cases long-term) interests in economic justice.

The fact that labor unions aren't ideological organizations doesn't, however, mean that individuals and organizations with specific political ideologies haven't historically and don't currently play a role in building them. To put it another way, different sorts of ideological organizations, particularly on the political Left, may regard labor unions either as a means to advance their own agendas or as an expression of an impulse among workers they believe to be critical to support. The distinction between these last two orientations—unions as a means to advance one's own agenda versus unions as an expression of an impulse they believe to be critical to support—is paramount. The first orientation is one of opportunism; the second is strategic and principled. We'll return to this point later in this section.

THE PROBLEM OF THE "OUTSIDE AGITATOR"

Central to the employer class's ideology is the notion that conditions in most workplaces are the equivalent of a family and should be treated as such. The employer envisions himself/herself as the head of the family, tends to have a patronizing attitude toward the work-ers, and believes that he or she (the employer) can settle any and all problems that may emerge. By definition, they disregard the notion that there is a built-in power conflict between workers and the employer class, even if that conflict need not be explosive in every case.

It's important to understand this frame of mind because what comes next only makes sense if you grasp the employer's assumption. For the employer class, any disruption among the workers *must* be the result of outside intervention since there's nothing in the work environment—as far as they're concerned—that should result in any significant problems. This method of thinking is called *sophistry,* and it can be summarized as a way of thinking that at first glance appears to be logical except the premise is flawed.[1]

The employer class isn't the only group that thinks this way. In struggles against racist discrimination, for instance, those who perpetrate such oppression always suggest that so-called outside elements have been involved.[2] Likewise, in struggles around gender discrimination, outside elements are regularly charged as being at the source of disrupting the supposedly harmonious relationship between men and women that had previously existed. Certainly, in the Arab democratic uprisings of 2011—sometimes referenced as the "Arab Spring"—the charge of "outside agitators" was regularly thrown around by the dictators as a way of deflecting criticism.

In employer/worker relations, the matter of outside agitators carries with it the suggestion of subversive ends. Part of this is because some revolutionary political organizations see workers as the base that is necessary for fundamental social transformation. But the critical element is that it is an often successful means for the employer to split the workers and blame individuals for alleged disruptive activity.

The charge of "outside agitator" also offers the employer the opportunity to delegitimize the concerns and activities of the workers themselves, particularly if the employer can find, among the workers, some who will support the cause of the employer. The story line can go any number of ways, including the employer spreading rumors about the alleged motives of workers who are organizing or connections they might have to supposed subversive elements. But it might not even be as strong as suggesting subversive ties; it may be enough to plant the idea that someone from among the workers does not *want* to work things out in-house but is turning instead to a *third party*.[3]

Insofar as employers were able to convince the broader public that unionization efforts were the result of nefarious outside actors, they could justify utilizing extreme measures to suppress organizing efforts. Such extreme measures included the use of the state militia (National Guard) as well as paid agents, such as elements associated with the notorious Pinkerton Company.

You may be wondering whether, nevertheless, there were/are outside forces. In truth, in many cases, there were and are organizers who have involved themselves in helping workers get organized. An organizer brings in knowledge and the experience of helping workers *who wish to organize* get organized (including providing information about labor law). That's their role. They don't substitute for the workers, but can be catalysts. In other cases, workers will organize on their own, with or without outside assistance.

When I was a labor organizer in Massachusetts years ago, I was generally contacted by workers who had already decided they wanted a labor union. This was not particularly strategic (from the standpoint of the union), but because they found out that my union, District 65 of the United Auto Workers, was organizing child-care and human-service-agency workers—and was relatively successful at it—many workers in those or similar agencies gravitated toward the union. In those cases, I would meet with the workers, explain the details of forming a labor union and bargaining a contract, and would proceed to assist them.

In many cases, organizers from a labor union (or some other labor organization) will approach workers who have not already decided to form or join a labor union. Then, organizers will seek out leaders or key opinion makers from among the workers to ascertain whether there really is a basis for organizing. Sometimes there is, and other times there isn't.

I have had the experience, for instance, of being contacted by workers who were interested in organizing. I spent a considerable amount of time with them, but we could not win because a core of workers simply did not think that a union was necessary. This sort of thing can happen, whether the employer gets involved or not (more about that later).

There are situations where workers will start organizing in the absence of any outside assistance. In the early 1990s, a clear example of that were the spontaneous strikes and organizing that took place among drywall construction workers in Southern California. After they had carried out a series of strikes, they joined the Carpenters Union, but they had begun organizing without the direct assistance of a union.

All of this begs an important question: is there something wrong with the idea of someone from the "outside" assisting workers in getting organized? There are different ways to think about this question, but keep in mind that on a regular basis there are things that you've done which occurred through "outside" influence. You may never have gone to a specific college—or college at all—had it not been for a recruiter that happened to visit your high school or perhaps you wouldn't have bought a house had it not been for a real estate agent helping you think through your needs and ability to pay. The bottom line is that there's nothing wrong with an "outsider" getting involved.

There is also another reason, one that is often more difficult to articulate, about why an outside "force" or individual can be important. Simply put, circumstances can often surround you to the extent to which you see no alternatives to your situation. Think of a dramatic scenario, such as an abusive relationship between two individuals. The abuse may have gone on for so long that it feels normal, and the abused person may think there's nothing he or she can do to prevent it. It may only be when there is an "outsider" who offers a different vantage point that things begin to change. But it does not have to be that dramatic. Let's say that you were living in an apartment building that had an infestation of roaches. If everyone's apartment had roaches, and if the owner or manager of the apartments treated that as normal, you might get used to it, not to say that you would like it.

It is under circumstances such as these that an "outsider" can often provide a different point of view. In other words, she can help you recognize that there are alternatives to your situation. The "threat" of so-called outside agitators is that they offer hope to those who have gone without it.

WHAT ABOUT THOSE RADICALS?

Since the English Civil War in the 1600s and the French Revolution a century later, there have been political forces that concerned themselves with and centered themselves on the struggles of working people. Following the French Revolution, most of these forces came to be identified as the political "Left."[4] By the 1800s, in Europe, in the United States, and, over time, in other parts of the world, these forces of the political Left not only organized among working people but also created theories to explain the situation facing working people. This largely derived from working people being the majority or significant minority of most countries, the role they played in the economy, and the level of oppression they faced. Two of the foremost theorists—but by no means the only such theorists—were Karl Marx and Friedrich Engels.[5]

Time and space do not permit a lengthy explanation of the theories of Marx and Engels, and there are many books on the subject. What is important to appreciate, however, is that their followers, some who designated themselves "socialists" and others "commu-

nists," believed the working class to be the central force in transforming society and ending all forms of oppression common to
capitalism (and any remnants of feudalism).

Organizations and individuals on the Left involved themselves
in helping form labor unions, often playing a critical role. But in
playing this role, they were building organizations that were not
ideological organizations even if the organizations took positions
on different matters. At the end of the day, membership in a union
did not require that a worker hold to a specific set of ideological
beliefs.

"Stop!" you might yell, if you are up on your labor history. What
about groups like the Industrial Workers of the World, which was
deeply ideological and didn't believe in capitalism?!

That is true, to an extent. The IWW, founded in 1905, was led
by revolutionary syndicalists, who believed that capitalism needed
to be replaced by a different system in which the unions and
workers were in control. Yet, the activity of the unions that were
formed was focused on the immediate needs of the workers who
were being organized, whether one was discussing mine workers in the West, agricultural workers in the fields, or dockworkers
in busy ports. To join the IWW, you didn't have to subscribe to the
beliefs of the leadership any more than joining a religious institution necessarily means that you adhere to the views of the leader of
the congregation.

What was different about the IWW, however, and what distinguished them from most of the unions of the American Federation of Labor, was their feistiness and their intolerance to racism.
The feistiness of the IWW, their willingness to get into a fight for
workers, the courage of their organizers, all of this made the IWW
legendary and made some of the songs that arose out of the IWW's
activity a part of union folklore. But it was also their opposition to
racism, something we shall discuss later, which gave them a special place in labor history. At the time of the birth of Jim Crow, they
would not tolerate segregated labor organizations.

These characteristics of the IWW flowed from their ideology. But that did not mean that subscribing to the ideology of the leadership became a prerequisite for membership. It is true that some labor organizations—usually not formal unions—have been created that hold to a specific ideology but, among other things, making an ideology the basis for membership in a union where that union is the exclusive representative of the workers for purposes of collective bargaining is illegal. More importantly, keeping a labor organization that is trying to reach masses of workers ideological nearly guarantees that it will remain small except during unusual times.

Employers were so fearful of the IWW that they began what can only be described as the *persecution* of the organization.[6] An entire set of statutes known as "criminal syndicalism laws" were put into effect with the purpose of smashing the IWW. What was at stake was never *whether* the IWW constituted a threat to US capitalism but rather whether it represented a pole of labor strength that could, over time, alter the political and economic landscape.

Had only the IWW been repressed, some might conclude that the employer class was simply worried about one group or even one tendency. But this was not the case. Other unions that were not connected to the IWW, such as the United Mine Workers of America, faced varying degrees of repression whether their leaders were socialists, communists, anarcho-syndicalists, or simply militant trade unionists.

For this reason, the fear of communists and other radicals has been a red herring—no pun intended—that has been used to confuse the broader public, promote panic, and justify the exercise of force as a means of eliminating social movements and organizations that might alter the balance of wealth and power in favor of working-class people.

During the 1930s, a great labor leader—who also happened to be a Republican—John L. Lewis, after being at odds with communists in the United Mine Workers, was prepared to openly ally with them in the building of what came to be known as the Congress of

Industrial Organizations (CIO). Lewis hired communists, socialists, and other leftists, recognizing quite openly that they were among the most committed and capable of the organizers that he could find for the mission of building a new union movement. He and others permitted unions to emerge in the CIO that were led by communists, socialists, and left-wing sympathizers. And while this was happening, labor was actually growing as a force in US society. It is important to realize that at no time was Lewis himself a communist or anything approaching that. He, nevertheless, recognized that the communists and other socialists knew how to get the job done, were good at uniting workers, had credibility (often because of their antiracism) with segments of the workforce that were skeptical of organized labor, and were not doing this work for the money.

So, it is true that leftists have often played a major and largely positive role in the union movement, including to this day. They haven't done this through manipulation but have done this work, whether as a rank-and-file activist, leader, or staff member, within the overall constraints of unions.

The sad truth is that in the late 1940s when, as a result of the beginning of the Cold War mass hysteria that gripped the country with a fear of communists (and other leftists), leftists were purged from the CIO in large numbers and organized labor began to stumble. The 1946–1951 effort at organizing the South—"Operation Dixie"— failed for many reasons, one being the fear by the campaign's leaders of the role of communists in the project. Thus, contrary to the experience from the 1930s, when communists and other leftists were welcomed into organizing campaigns, in 1946, this was quite different. The campaign failed miserably, though those unions in the South led by leftists tended to fare better than others, at least initially.

Radicals on the political Left, therefore, constitute one of the currents within trade unionism. An accurate look at labor history demonstrates that left-wing activists in the unions were often central in the building and rebuilding of the labor movement, irrespective of their longer-term views. Suggesting that unions are somehow inappropriate due to the activities of leftists misses a central organizational fact about unions: they are open to workers of any number of political tendencies. Any effort to eliminate someone due to their political tendency will have a cascading effect, as was demonstrated during the Cold War, where the hunt for radicals became a means to suppress dissent within the union movement itself.

"UNIONS ARE ALL RACIST AND PEOPLE OF COLOR NEED NOT APPLY."

Communities of color have a complicated relationship with organized labor—one that stems from a history that includes examples of courageous interracial/interethnic solidarity on the one hand and intense racial/ethnic antagonism on the other.

To address this charge, it's critical to appreciate three underlying problems: the character of the United States as a political entity, the implications of competition among workers, and social control over workers by the employer class.

THE BIG PICTURE

To say that unions are racist is a problematic assertion and first necessitates understanding that race is a sociopolitical concept rather than a matter of either biology or imagination. In the past twenty years, there has been a proliferation of literature on the subject,[1] but I'll outline several relevant points:

- This country began as a settler state intent on removing the indigenous population. There was no significant attempt to build a bond between the settlers and the indigenous population.[2]
- Africans, as well as Europeans, were brought to North America as indentured servants, meaning they could achieve freedom

after a specific period of time. Africans were also brought
as slaves.

· In response to regular revolts of indentured servants that were
  often composed of both European and African (and sometimes
  Native American) laborers, indentured servitude for Africans
  was fully replaced by slavery-for-life by the late 1600s.

· "Race" was constructed in the 1600s as a mechanism that
  enabled those in power to divide and conquer. It wasn't just
  the proliferation of a set of bad ideas but the combination of
  certain ideas (such as the inferiority/superiority of certain
  groups) with concrete practices that reinforced the suppression of certain groups.

· "Race" has never been a hard and fast category because certain groups that were, for example, not considered white in
  a given era, e.g., the Irish of the 1700s, "became" white in a
  different era, e.g., the mid- to late 1800s. This evolution is
  a reflection of politics, not biology.[3]

· White workers are taught to prioritize their racial identity as
  white over their reality as part of the laboring classes and later
  as part of the working class.

· As a consequence, every institution in the United States was
  corrupted by the stench of racism, a fact demonstrated time and
  again by the differential in treatment various groups received,
  e.g., access to land, education, housing, jobs, and security.

The second issue concerns competition among workers. In the
beginning of this book, I discussed competition for jobs and benefits that exists among workers. When workers respond to such
competition, they do so in one of two ways. The first is a technique
known as "exclusion" in which you minimize the number of individuals you're attempting to organize to guarantee that those who
succeed benefit significantly. An example of this would be the old
guilds or many of the building trades unions. Both organizations
want to ensure that the labor market for their particular craft or

trade isn't flooded, so they create membership requirements that ensure members are skilled and that the market isn't overloaded.

"Exclusion" doesn't necessarily mean racist or sexist; it can result from a sober analysis of the labor market and the nature of the job. In either case, it's one option. The alternative is "inclusion," which aims to organize all that can be organized. This may mean not only the existing workforce for a particular employer, but all workers in that industry. It may even go further and seek to organize those who are potential members of this job market.

Although the inclusion/exclusion dichotomy doesn't necessarily break down on a racial/ethnic basis, in the United States, it typically does. As a result, it has—historically—been common to have certain components of a union dominated by particular racial or ethnic groups. It has also been common to find entire industries missing a critical mass of women. In the building trades, for instance, there might be in the same city a local union that's known as an "Italian" local and another known as an "Irish" local because of the ethnic character of the leadership and the dominant demographics of the local union itself.

The inclusion/exclusion dichotomy provides a framework for understanding how competition can be addressed by workers. When you take into account race and ethnicity, these can become the sources of identity—rather than a collective identity as "workers." As a result, race and ethnicity can be used to determine whose experiences, life, and suffering is relevant versus those who are considered irrelevant or secondary. This reality explains some of the tensions that exist between many building trades unions and communities of color. For instance, in Boston a local union of the Ironworkers didn't have any members of color for most of the twentieth century. They were, in effect, not permitted to join.[4] It was only through a courageous lawsuit by several black ironworkers in 1972 that entrance was opened. It should, therefore, come as no surprise that Boston communities of color tended to view the building trades as racist and inaccessible.

7/16/2020 10:20 7/10

FIDLER MICHAEL D

Item Number: 31901051551960

Join Summer Reading, June 6 - August 6.
Go to: ccclib.org/summer. All Contra Costa
County Libraries will be closed on July 3rd
and July 4th. Items may be renewed at
ccclib.org or by calling 1-800-984-4636, menu
option 1. Book drops will be open.

Hold Shelf Slip

But there is another side to this story. Many white members of these building trades unions tended to look at membership as their familial inheritance and legacy. In their minds, their fathers or uncles may have been members of the same craft union, and as a result, they view union membership as a passing of the torch. Additionally, like any other worker, they need an income so, from their standpoint, workers of color have not paid their "dues" and should wait their turn.

To get to the bottom of this tension, one must understand history. The white building trades' worker may be completely oblivious to the historic exclusion of workers of color. In this sense, they want to uphold a privileged place in the workforce rather than acknowledging that dog-eat-dog competition benefits no one. To the extent to which they put blinders on and refuse to look at history, they deceive themselves by believing that *they* are somehow the victims, thereby contributing to the further division among workers and the weakening of their power.

This actually takes us to the third issue—social control. The idea of social control was the preoccupation of Theodore Allen in his study of race in North America. As Allen expertly demonstrates, the introduction of "race" wasn't an accident or the result of some genetic historic tension; it was constructed with particular objectives in mind. The repeated uprisings in the colonial North America of the 1600s unnerved the ruling elite. To ensure the suppression of the uprisings, they required a military force, but more importantly, they needed to foment divisions within the rebellious ranks of the laboring population. "Race" then became a means of exacerbating the divisions that capitalism had already engendered within the workforce by giving them a new identity (and a set of consequences when challenged).

What's important in understanding these divisions is that they are both structurally and ideologically reinforced. For example, the textile industry in the South for years restricted the entrance of black workers to only the least skilled positions. Additionally, other industries have placed workers of color in the most danger-ous jobs, such as in steel manufacturing where African Americans and Chicanos would often be located. But it also plays itself out in retail where many of the front-of-the-store positions are reserved for whites.

These divisions can be so intense that they undermine any chance of organizing to improve the quality of life for the work-force. Former Major League Baseball Players Association executive director Marvin Miller described one such example:

> When [Jackie] Robinson made his major league debut, there was talk among the players of organizing a *strike* [emphasis in original]: Apparently, players who didn't have enough sense of purpose to unite and organize for their own improved condi-tions were ready to strike to keep blacks off the field. And to go one step further, prior to 1966, the same was true of the Play-ers Association organization. It was a company-dominated outfit with no real structure and had never had a black player representative. . . . It should come as no surprise that by the mid-1960s blacks and Latin players didn't have confidence that the Players Association was any different than before or, for that matter, different from other organizations and insti-tutions in America.[5]

As Miller noted, the white players were prepared to go to war to re-strict the entrance of black players but proved largely incapable of organizing themselves to improve *their own* conditions. What Miller describes was the subservience of most players to the owners. In other words, they were prepared to restrict the racial/ethnic turf of baseball, while at the same time were willing to accept the uncon-ditional domination of the sport by the owners who were running them into the ground. This "compromise" signaled that owners had secured social control.

WERE WORKERS OF COLOR IRRELEVANT IN THE BUILDING OF UNIONS?

Until the early 1970s, one would've thought that workers of color were largely bystanders in the creation of unions. Led by historians such as Philip S. Foner, labor history was reexamined, and facts about workers of color that had been ignored or were previously unknown were uncovered. Here are a few interesting tidbits:

- The 1600s were rocked by revolts of laboring people in which black laborers played a critical role (e.g., Bacon's Rebellion).
- The early years of Reconstruction[6] witnessed the emergence of unions and unionlike organizations among the freed African laborers in the South, many of which engaged in what we'd today term "wildcat strikes."[7]
- Black dockworkers organized throughout the South from the mid to late nineteenth century and well into the twentieth century.
- Latino and Native American mine workers were a key part of the Industrial Workers of the World's efforts in the Southwest.
- Asian American workers also had to organize separately from whites because they were excluded and were often the targets of some of the most virulently racist campaigns. In the early twentieth century, there was a unified effort of Japanese and Mexican American workers called the Japanese-Mexican Labor Association. Asian American workers would go on to play a major role in organizing in agriculture and canneries.
- The success of the CIO was largely based on the support that the CIO unions were able to win among African Americans, Chicanos and Asian American workers in key industries. These groups often represented the key ingredient to success.

There is much here that could be discussed, but the point is that for years this history was largely ignored. It wasn't simply that workers of color found themselves excluded from certain unions, but rather, that most of the *official movement* excluded this history. Because this history was ignored, many workers of color had no sense of their own centrality to the development of the labor movement.

Knowing this history helps one realize that matters are not one-sided. In other words, to those who say that unions are racist, one can reply that there's certainly a history of racism, but it's also the case that there are countless examples of antiracist organizing and solidarity.

TODAY'S SITUATION

The realities of race and labor today are both surprising and yet not so shocking given this tumultuous history. In 2010, among major race and ethnicity groups, black workers were more likely to be union members (13.4 percent) than were white (11.7 percent), Asian American (10.9 percent), or Latino (10.0 percent) workers.[8] Latinos are the fastest growing segment of the unionized workforce, moving from 5.8 percent in 1983 to 12.2 percent in 2008. Asian Americans have also grown in the unionized workforce, from 2.5 percent in 1989 to 4.6 percent in 2008. Black workers are about 13 percent of the unionized workforce, a percentage that has not changed much since 1983.[9]

There are a number of conclusions that we can draw from these statistics. First, and for many most surprisingly, the percentage of African American union members (that is, as a percentage of African Americans) has consistently outpaced other racial/ethnic groups for years. The percentage of African Americans who were union members (compared with the percentage of union members who are African American) has dropped from roughly 18 percent about ten years ago to its current 13.4 percent, more than likely representing the combination of the hits taken in unionized manufacturing as well as the reduction in the public sector workforce. That said, this percentage is illustrative of a larger tendency, that is, African Americans are more likely to be pro-union than most other groups, a fact that most union organizers will corroborate. In fact, it's not just union organizers who recognize this. Employers have often shaped their own hiring policies around how to avoid black workers, and not simply for traditionally racist reasons.[10]

While there are significant numbers of workers of color who are members of labor unions, this doesn't extend to the top leadership and staff of most unions. In fact, the demand for greater representation at the top dates back to the 1930s, but took a more organized form with the creation of the National Negro Labor Council, beginning in around 1951.[11] While such insurgencies have altered many policies of organized labor to make them more amiable to workers of color, there has been immense difficulty cracking into the upper echelon. The reasons for this problem include the following:

- *Straight demographics.* Union elections include all members. It's winner take all, unless the constitution of the union provides for a certain percentage of slots for people of color. Thus, a demographic minority may find it difficult to break in.
- *Favoritism.* In top staff positions, a tendency by top leaders to favor people they know. This may not be consciously racist, but the result is the same, i.e., an overreliance on the same pool of people and a reluctance to take "risks" with outsiders or unknowns.
- *Source pools.* This is related to the last item, but the pools for certain positions are often ones that have limited numbers of applicants of color.
- *Straight-out racism.* The belief that these top positions simply shouldn't be occupied by people of color (rationales such as "they are not ready," or "they are not qualified"). This may play out in an almost oligarchic manner, in which a small group reproduces itself.

In response to these challenges, union members of color and their allies have often organized caucuses to demand changes in internal and external policies, including hiring policies. But there is intense resistance to the idea of ensuring that a certain percentage of leadership positions are designated for people of color. This, then, results in a strange situation in which union members of color find themselves often excluded from leadership positions; white leaders declare that they can represent everyone, irrespective of race; and union members of color then become alienated and either drop away or resist. It's possible that some changes may be introduced, but these don't necessarily alter power relationships. Yet the union represents many of the core interests of that same alienated segment of the membership, creating a dilemma as to how to move forward.

It's true that union staffs and leaderships have become more diverse over the last twenty-five years, but this diversity doesn't necessarily mean that the internal power relationships have fundamentally shifted. The question is always one of *who* is actually making the decisions, not just who is at the table. This is one of the biggest challenges facing unions as they proceed into the twenty-first century.

"UNIONS HAVE A HISTORY OF SEXISM . . . WHAT MAKES THEM BETTER NOW?"

As with allegations of racism in unions, charges of sexism, while often speaking to very real problems and injustices, can also be used—when stated broadly and without specification—as a means to promote an atmosphere of cynicism and despair.

WOMEN, WEALTH, AND WORK

The rise of patriarchal society has a long and varied history. In general, matrilineal societies, those led by women where identity and inheritance was based on the mother, were overthrown and replaced not by coequal arrangements but with male domination. Wealth was expropriated from women along with independent societal power.[1]

As capitalism developed, the role of women in work wasn't entirely consistent; however, work was divided into two parts. There was formal work, that is, activity that was largely accepted as "work." Separately there were nonformal work activities like child rearing and household maintenance that, as capitalism developed, weren't regarded as proper work but simply as part of women's domain. In agricultural societies, there were gender divisions of labor, but with the evolution of manufacturing, certain jobs were reserved for women and others for men. The textile industry, which relied on the labor power of women, is an illustrative case. However, increasingly the formal activity of men was given greater societal importance than women's labor.

The idea that "men run the family, and women run the house" was a glib way of describing a fundamental power imbalance: whereas the activities of reproducing the family and keeping it stable were largely placed before women, men were seen as the breadwinners, as the wage-based economy came to replace all other economic forms.

Certainly, by the 1800s, the outside-the-home activity of women came to be seen as supplemental to the income brought in by men. This was certainly the case for married women. Thus, it should be no surprise that labor unions developed as largely male-dominated organizations and remained so well into the twentieth century. There were, nevertheless, specific activities that were largely reserved for women, not all of which was considered by the dominant society to be "real work." Textile and garment work had a significant female workforce and would become the site of very progressive union organizing in the twentieth century. Agricultural and domestic work weren't generally legitimized, and in the case of agriculture, the work of the family (including the children) wasn't seen as an equitable cooperative but instead, a male-led organism.

By the late nineteenth and early twentieth centuries, a concept developed known as the "family wage," or the notion that a man should receive a wage sufficient to support a wife and children. Although there were women who supported this concept, in effect what it institutionalized was the notion that men's work should be the defining feature in society and within any family.

WOMEN'S CONTRIBUTION TO UNIONS

One of the most fascinating facts of labor history—and ignored for years—is that women have been central to it from the beginning. Much like the history of workers of color, until twenty-five to thirty years ago, the history of women in unions was treated as largely marginal,[2] yet nothing could be further from the truth. Consider the following examples:

- 1824: Women weavers and men strike in Pawtucket, Rhode Island.
- 1825: Lavinia Waight and Louise Mitchell form the United Tailoresses Society and lead a strike. This was the first example of women striking on their own.
- 1829: Women millworkers in Taunton, Massachusetts, strike.
- 1834: Women in Lowell, Massachusetts, strike over firings.
- 1836: Factory Girls Association leads strike of 1,500 in Lowell. Similar strikes take place in New York and Pennsylvania.
- 1866: In Jackson, Mississippi, black washerwomen resolve to charge the same rate for their work.
- 1867: Cigar Makers Union is the first national union to accept women as members.
- 1869: Daughters of St. Crispin, founded in Lynn, Massachusetts, becomes the first national women's labor organization.
- 1869: Mary A. S. Carey addresses the convention of the Colored National Labor Union.
- 1877: "Mother Jones" supports striking railroad workers and goes on to a long career in the labor movement.
- 1881: 3,000 black washerwomen in Atlanta go on strike.
- 1886: The Knights of Labor[3] sets up a women's department.
- 1892: The American Federation of Labor hires its first female organizer.
- 1909: "Uprising of the 20,000," in which women shirtwaist workers mobilize en masse and join unions.[4]

And this is only through 1909! To this could certainly be added many more examples, including, in the twentieth century, the role of Chicano and Mexicano women in the CIO's organizing of the Southwest in the 1930s and 1940s; the organizing of African American domestic workers in the 1940s; the Charleston, South Carolina, hospital workers' strike of 1969, led by African American women (and deeply linked with the civil rights movement); the role of Chicanas in the Farah strike in the Southwest in the 1970s; and the role of Latinas generally in the Watsonville cannery strike of the 1980s.[5]

If we examine the pre-1909 examples, we can draw a number of conclusions. First and foremost, these examples reveal that early manufacturing in New England relied heavily on the labor power of women. Although the work was segregated by gender, there were repeated strikes and other worker mobilizations that involved both men and women.

A second critical point, and one worth reiterating, is that women's activism corresponded to the rise of the union movement as a whole. In other words, the emergence of an identifiable union movement can't be credited to men organizing alone or first, but rather, the upsurge of both men *and* women workers.

A third point that is contained in depth in the pre-1909 list was the dynamic and complicated relationship between the women's suffrage movement and the union movement. Thus, famous suffragists like Susan B. Anthony could on the one hand support unions and women's membership only to later fall out with trade unionists by suggesting that women consider "scabbing" a strike (crossing picket lines). In either case, the union movement tended to support equal pay for equal work as one of its platforms, and there were many suffragists who recognized the importance of trade unionism and the role that women could play in it.

A fourth point we can draw is that women workers were quite prepared to go it alone, if necessary. Part of this is credited to the segregated nature of work in which entire areas in a factory (or in a sector of the economy) would be all women. But more importantly, the courage and determination of the women clashed with the societal portrayal of women as helpless figures that had to be taken care of.

Fifth, what isn't as obvious unless you know something about the industries involved is that the women's work was itself segregated based on race. The textile plants in the Northeast became a melting pot of immigrant workers, and particularly immigrant women workers, while African Americans and other workers of color were excluded. As evidenced by the 1866 strike of black washerwomen, there was a tendency to allocate service and agricultural work to black women.

Finally, the history of women workers of color is often segregated itself. The examples of women workers of color and their struggles and the roles they played has been regularly ignored or understudied both when one is examining the history of women workers as well as when one is examining the history of workers of color.

As more labor unions were created in the twentieth century, women were welcomed in some settings and rejected in others. Where they were welcomed, they tended to be segregated, at least in the beginning. And even in situations where entire unions had a significant, if not majority, female membership, men tended to dominate the leadership. This latter point has resulted in struggles to this day.

MORE RECENTLY

Today women make up 45 percent of unionized workers, up from 35 percent in 1983.[6] Karen Nussbaum, founder of the women workers' organization 9-to-5 and a leader in the AFL-CIO, has noted that organized labor represents the largest movement of women in the United States. The fact that we tend not to think about it that way speaks to the challenges faced within the union movement itself.

While it was the case that, beginning in the nineteenth century, the male-dominated union movement began creating staff openings for women, these openings were inconsistent and limited. It took more than ten years for the AFL to hire its first female organizer. For the Knights of Labor before them, there was a willingness to have women as components of the movement, but to keep them segregated nevertheless. In addition, while it was true that unions would express their support for the *principle* of equal pay for equal work, this didn't necessarily translate into an active campaign by male labor leaders or activists.

Throughout the twentieth century, an equally significant matter has been women's entry into job markets from which they were previously excluded, along with the challenge of preventing the elimination of women from various jobs. To a great extent, the union movement treated the gender division of labor as insurmountable. In some cases, it was encoded in the forms of organization that were created. Labor scholar Dorothy Sue Cobble wrote about one such formation, the waitresses union that operated within the larger Hotel Employees and Restaurant Employees International Union.[7] Additionally, certain other forms of organization were created to address women workers, such as the Women's Trade Union League. But what was rare was the union movement struggling to break down doors that had restricted women. It is important to note that when it came to race, this was also rare.[8] Of equal importance was the failure to defend women workers from removal when men were reentering the workforce after World War II. This historic episode is one that is rarely discussed, even by women who were directly affected by it. Yet, it was traumatizing to the victims and reveals a great deal about how women and work were regarded at that time.

When the United States entered World War II, the massive troop mobilization created a radical shift in the perception of women and work. Almost overnight, the rhetoric changed from women taking care of the home to women replacing men at jobs from which they'd been excluded. It even extended to the field of sports, as dramatized in the fact-based 1992 film *A League of Their Own* where a women's baseball league was established in response to the number of men who were no longer available to play baseball. In either case, when returning male veterans went back to work, the women who had been successfully occupying those jobs were released, that is, purged. Much as in the end of *A League of Their Own*, many women affected by the purge refused to discuss it for the rest of their lives and went into denial. Society rearranged itself and justified this purge, suggesting that what had taken place during World War II was a temporary phenomenon. While that may have been the case, it did set in motion various events that would contribute to the rise of a new women's movement some years later.

When it comes to both race and gender, the union movement has great difficulty determining to what extent it should challenge existing structural practices. When the Steel Workers Organizing Committee (which later became the United Steelworkers of America) was actively organizing in the 1930s, it would frequently organize workers without changing or challenging the racial dynamics of a given workplace. Therefore, while the living standard of the workers would increase, the conditions and location of work generally remained segregated according to race. Much the same happened with women: organized labor either accepted the prevailing view (that is, men should be dominant), or it concluded that it wasn't the union's responsibility to challenge established practices and instead should focus on improving the conditions of the workers given the constraints applied. From this standpoint, if workers were segregated by gender, it was only the union's objective to improve the conditions of the workers in their respective segregated conditions. In effect, much of labor's leadership was prepared to accept key elements of the status quo while at the same time fighting to improve the lives of women!

As a result of this contradiction, beginning in the 1970s, women and their male allies placed increased pressure on the officialdom of organized labor seeking changes in the manner in which the unions operated. Again, similar to the fight for racial equality, activists sought to increase the numbers of women in leadership and on staff. There were also demands for the unions to address more concretely issues that disproportionately affected women. Important changes became noticeable in the 1980s and 1990s, when some unions, for instance, not only took up issues of equal pay for equal work but also something that came to be known as "comparable worth." This is a form of pay equity that identifies the fact that gender segregation created a situation in which jobs done by women weren't identical to those done by men, but represented equivalent roles in an organization. Additionally, unions began taking up other issues such as child care and matters of health care that particularly affected women.

During this period, more women were elected to leadership positions, though the top positions remained largely with men. The women who gained tended to be white, a fact that became a source of additional tension but also mirrored a phenomenon taking place in other sectors of society, which saw that some of the chief beneficiaries of affirmative action and affirmative action–type efforts were white women.

This all returns us, however, to the problem raised by Karen Nussbaum. With a union movement that is 45 percent female, it's curious that it doesn't see itself as a part of the women's movement. This has to be additionally understood in the manner in which the union movement sees itself or self-identifies. To the extent to which the union movement narrows its self-identification to workplace economics and, specifically, to increasing the living standard of its existing (or even potential) members, it runs itself into a hole. It's not that economics is unimportant. On the contrary, it's critical, but the question remains: what's the relationship of the economic struggle (broadly defined) to other issues of injustice that face our members? In this case, women's struggles aren't exclusively economic, but one must ask to what extent the union movement should actively engage itself in the broader fight against injustice. For some male (and even female) union members, the answer has been not to engage at all, that is, to take a pass and describe such struggles as not being "union struggles." This point of view is erroneous and misses the opportunity to build more diverse allies and reframe unionism as an instrument for justice.

MYTH 14

"UNIONS DEAL WITH WAGES, HOURS, AND WORKING CONDITIONS; WHAT ABOUT OTHER ISSUES?"

The National Labor Relations Act (NLRA) grants most workers the opportunity to bargain over the terms and conditions of their employment. It lays out what can be legally bargained, what may be bargained if both sides agree (what are called "permissive subjects"), and areas that may not be bargained. The state of the law, however, doesn't reveal much in terms of what unions *can* do.

BARGAINING

Unions can bargain over wages, hours, and working conditions. That means they can legally put together proposals in those areas, and such proposals must be considered by management and bargained in good faith. This *doesn't* mean management must agree with the union's proposals any more than the union must agree with management's proposals. But there must be evidence of good faith bargaining, otherwise one side may be charged by the National Labor Relations Board (the labor relations court) with an *unfair labor practice*.[1]

The second category, mentioned above, is that of "permissive" subjects for bargaining. Essentially, there are a set of subjects that can be bargained if both sides agree. They aren't illegal, but they can't be bargained to impasse, which is to say they can't be issues that are taken to an arbitrator or around which a strike is organized.

The third category is that which the law considers to be illegal. In other words, in bargaining you can't get around a statute that has declared something illegal, such as racial discrimination, by bargaining a discriminatory provision in your collective bargaining agreement.

What's particularly important to know, however, is that the law doesn't put ownership up for debate or mandatory bargaining. In 1946, the United Auto Workers attempted to get the automobile manufacturers to bargain for workers' voice in management, but this was rejected. Since that time, nearly all collective bargaining agreements have something called a "management rights clause." This ominous sounding provision is generally at the beginning of every collective bargaining agreement and directly outlines what management can do, also stating matters that management has no intention of negotiating. It essentially says, *We run this operation and will not let you tell us how to run it. You aren't involved in management, investments, or any of the key business decisions, so don't even think about it.*

This can seem discouraging particularly if you realize that economic justice isn't simply a matter of a wage or a salary, or the conditions of work, but has more to do with how a company or organization is run and the way that society operates. This brings us back to ownership and control. Capitalism doesn't accept that those who work should have a legitimate role in the running of an organization. It doesn't necessarily forbid it, mind you, but it doesn't regard this as grounds for equitable negotiations.[2]

When a very vibrant union movement in 1946 reached this impasse, the movement largely retreated and opted to make the best out of the situation by bargaining over wages, hours, and working conditions (rather than pressing this struggle in other arenas). This isn't the only decision that they could've made, but it is one that brought with it significant consequences in terms of narrowing the vision of the movement.

AND?

Unions haven't restricted themselves to addressing issues of wages, hours, and working conditions, but have involved themselves in a variety of activities. The Knights of Labor, a major labor movement of the late nineteenth century, included worker cooperatives and social clubs. Prior to the introduction of genuine insurance programs, many unions initiated their own versions often called "death benefit" provisions. Today, unions often offer special benefit programs for members and their families, including automobile purchasing programs, scholarships, disaster relief, various discounts on merchandise, and internal educational initiatives. In fact, the AFL-CIO sponsors its own college, the National Labor College, targeting the educational needs of working people.

Unions also address matters of policy and legislation. Often, this work by unions directly responds to the needs of the economic sector a particular union operates in, but that isn't always the case. At the level of central labor councils, state federations, and the national AFL-CIO, the union movement may address broader issues facing working people. For example, although the union movement was divided over how to respond to the civil rights movement of the 1950s through the 1970s, the national AFL-CIO did endorse the Civil Rights Act of 1964. Unions took stands, both pro and con, on the Vietnam War. During the 1980s, large segments of the U.S. union movement mobilized against the white supremacist apartheid regime in South Africa.

Today, some unions have become very involved with environmental concerns. As a whole, the union movement has involved itself in trade policy (for example, the fight over the North American Free Trade Agreement), and some of the more visionary unions have involved themselves in matters of economic development, as was seen with the United Steelworkers of America pact with the Mondragon cooperatives of the Basque region of Spain.[3]

All of this suggests that there's a wide breadth of activity, so though the specific matter of bargaining may be restricted, unions nevertheless can engage in the cause of broader justice if they so choose.

HOW AND WHY DO UNIONS GET INVOLVED IN OTHER ISSUES?

In the nineteenth century, the early union movement saw itself as addressing a host of needs facing workers. With workers' needs in mind, a federation (in this case, the Knights of Labor) that included unions and worker cooperatives was consistent with the union movement's raison d'être. Another approach central to the early movement's mission was to encourage workers to think in terms of the creation of local or national labor parties to address the political needs and demands of workers.

Under its founder, Samuel Gompers, the AFL began to reshape how mainstream trade unionism was understood. Gompers de-emphasized, and actually repudiated, the notion of the creation of a workers' or labor party, for instance. In addition, there was less interest in establishing independent worker institutions, though many did arise in the early twentieth century largely due to the efforts of European immigrants, and separately, workers of color with their own respective institutions. This is important to emphasize because restrictions on unions are often attributed to legislation, but what's truly at stake is the self-conception of the union itself.

Then how can you get your union involved in issues that go beyond wages, hours, and working conditions? The short answer is that you have to foster a sentiment within the union for those activities. There are few guideposts on what a union will address. If a matter falls within the broad realm of economic and/or social justice, a union can generally feel that addressing it is legitimate (even if there is disagreement on the issue itself). Technically, a resolution needs to be passed to endorse a specific activity or a cause, and then it's the leadership's responsibility to implement it.[4]

I recall in the 1980s, as the antiapartheid movement gained support, many activists concerned about South Africa wanted their unions to take up the issue. This ranged from supporting legislation calling for sanctions on the apartheid government to providing financial assistance to those involved in the struggle to supporting and often participating in local protests.

To get unions to address this issue, there first needed to be a core of people who believed in it. This core would then need to educate other members about South Africa and explain why it should be of any interest and importance to the union. Such an education effort could take any length of time until there was a critical mass of members who could bring the matter to a membership meeting, or in the case of a national/international union, convention.

However, simply because an issue is important to a large number of people inside or outside of a union doesn't guarantee that the issue will be taken up. In the case of South Africa, some individuals who opposed the involvement of US unions in the antiapartheid struggle did so out of a deep fear of the antiapartheid movement itself (especially a fear of the core component of the movement that was *within* South Africa). Fueled by Cold War mentalities and fears of alleged terrorism, some in the union movement preferred to remain silent in the face of the apartheid government's atrocities. There were others who, while ostensibly opposing apartheid, sought a middle path that didn't commit them to supporting the forces in South Africa (such as the African National Congress and the Pan Africanist Congress of Azania) fighting for freedom.

Given this, advocates for the antiapartheid movement had to develop their core arguments and build alliances until their position could prevail. Eventually an antiapartheid plank became something akin to the "common sense" position within the union movement. As a result, many union activists felt empowered to get involved in the larger antiapartheid movement representing their respective union.

Through internal discussion, debate, and lobbying, a union can become involved in any number of issues that go way beyond wages, hours, and working conditions. This all begs the question of why it's often so difficult to get a union to move beyond wages, hours, and working conditions.

To a great extent, the answer rests with Gompers and his conception of trade unionism. In narrowing the focus of unionism to a framework that came to be known as "pure and simple unionism" or "bread-and-butter unionism," the social vision that had accompanied the rise of labor unions began to vanish. The union became the equivalent of a business venture[5] in the sense that it functioned on a narrow interpretation of members' needs. These needs were tied in with particular companies or industries, and the circumstances that often trapped workers were not called into question.

Although at points Gompers had a broader view of the world and was an outspoken critic on various issues,[6] his vision of unionism didn't see itself at odds with the capitalist system or even with some of the most egregious elements of that system, such as Jim Crow segregation in the South.

Gompers "branded" the US union movement, and while it's true that alternative approaches to unionism emerged in the twentieth and the early twenty-first century (such as the Industrial Workers of the World and the CIO in the twentieth century), his imprint remains. One consequence of this lasting influence is that members will often be told, in response to suggestions that the union involve itself in addressing social and economic injustice, "What you are proposing is not a union issue." When the matter of South African apartheid was being raised in the United States, in fact, many union leaders suggested that it wasn't a union issue. In fact, prior to the Civil War, many Northern white union leaders argued that *slavery* wasn't an issue around which unions should offer an opinion.

When examining unions in this country and around the world it's clear that while their core work is generally focused on the conditions of the workforce, they can find themselves engaged in various activities. Here are some examples:

- In St. Louis, in the 1960s, a large local union of the Teamsters Union became directly involved in community organizing.
- In the 1950s and 1960s, the local union of the Packinghouse Workers in Boston, did the same, including having their shop stewards involved in community-based work.
- During the era of the civil rights movement, certain unions devoted significant resources to the fight against segregation and proved to be key allies of Dr. King and the Southern Christian Leadership Conference. Notable unions included District 65/Distributive Workers of America (which would later merge with the UAW), and Local 1199/National Union of Health and Hospital Workers (which would later split, with a portion joining the Service Employees International Union and the other joining the American Federation of State, County and Municipal Employees).
- The Mine, Mill, and Smelter Workers Union (which later merged with the United Steelworkers of America) helped form the Asociación National México-Americana to organize Chicanos in the Southwest.
- In the current era, the Service Employees International Union has started a "Fight for a Fair Economy" as a large-scale mobilization against the economic crisis.
- The national AFL-CIO has undertaken its own campaign around the demand for work, which has included the involvement of several central labor councils in the effort to organize unemployed workers.

The union, therefore, can be an instrument to pursue broader issues of social and economic justice, but it's critical to understand that most union limitations are self-imposed because of a specific ideology of trade unionism. This is of particular urgency today as economic crises continue to affect much of the advanced capitalist world. Restricting the union to the narrow confines of a workplace prevents it from having a broader influence.

A final point to note here concerns younger workers who often enter the workforce with little historical knowledge, or in some cases, don't know what a labor union actually is. It is, however, the case that many enter the labor union with clear ideas and some hopes for what unions can do to change the world only to be told, in one way or another, that their ideas have no place in the world of organized labor. Rather than truly listening to the younger workers, many older, veteran union members write off suggestions as naive and idealistic. A result of this dismissive response is alienation and declining membership.

This generational problem isn't unique to unions as many other nonprofit organizations and justice-oriented groups are grappling with something similar. Despite the crisis in which labor unions find themselves, there's frequently an unwillingness to change and discard old approaches. This means that the same methods used to rally union support for the South African antiapartheid movement in the 1970s and 1980s—building cores of people who uphold views of the need for change and winning over a larger constituency— must be implemented today if we want to bring about lasting change and the creation of a union movement relevant to the twenty-first century.

MYTH 15

"YES, UNIONS ARE GOOD FOR THEIR MEMBERS, BUT THEY HURT THE REST OF US!"

An interesting poll taken in the late 1990s revealed two note-worthy points.[1] First, the majority or near majority of non-union workers wanted to be in a union or a unionlike association.[2] The second, somewhat paradoxical point discussed at the time of the original poll in the 1990s within the AFL-CIO, was the perception—discussed by the pollsters—that unions were good for their members but not everyone else. Before addressing why unions are, in fact, good for most people, let's unpack this perception.

STEPPING BACKWARD

Something noticeable happened to unions beginning in the late 1940s and continuing through the early 1950s: they slowly began to distance themselves from social justice issues, or to put it in an-other way, from being a "cause." While Samuel Gompers had pro-moted a form of unionism that largely repudiated working class struggle for justice in favor of an accommodationist unionism in the interest of big business, this wasn't the only form of trade unionism on the terrain. There were opposing tendencies among trade unionists. Within these opposing tendencies, there was the sentiment of unionism as a "cause" that liberals, progressives, and all those interested in justice should support regardless of whether they were in unions themselves. For that matter, unions in the CIO were viewed as potential supporters of other social and economic justice struggles. A case in point was the relationship built between the CIO and the united front of black American organizations called the National Negro Congress during the late 1930s.

The broader identification with trade unionism played itself out in various ways including widespread refusal to cross picket lines. This was central to the culture in many parts of the country—you just didn't cross them. In fact, if you saw a picket line you would check to see whether it was an "informational picket line"[3] or the picket line for a strike. In the broader cultural realm this also played out in books and films where unions would be mentioned favorably, such as during World War II with films like Humphrey Bogart's *Action in the North Atlantic*.

It's important to appreciate that this wasn't purely ideological. The reality is that as labor unions gained in strength and numbers they affected society at large. The living standards of most workers began to climb prior to World War II and skyrocketed after the war. While there were, of course, larger economic factors that affected this like the United States' dominance in the capitalist world, one fact that's often ignored is that the division of domestic wealth would've been nowhere near what it was had it not been for organized workers.

Unions had influenced developments prior to this period, such as the establishment of the forty-hour workweek. In fact, the major changes that unfolded during the New Deal era were brought about through pressure from a very vital union movement. Two such changes included the Fair Labor Standards Act and Social Security. The union movement of the 1930s and 1940s not only pushed for reforms that benefitted their own members but also for larger societal initiatives.

After the Cold War purges of unions in the late 1940s, the atmosphere slowly began to change as more anticommunist demagogues insisted that a labor movement that talked about class, the struggle of the poor, and middle class against the wealthy was somehow subversive. It became worse as anticommunists suggested that those advocating desegregation and any degree of race mixing were also subversive, radical, and God-forbid, communists! The level of fear that was promoted, along with former allies turning against one another, led to a paralysis of both thought and action in the union movement. In the 1930s, the union movement—specifically the CIO—had been quite prepared to tackle racism in many sectors of the economy and unite with community groups from among people of color. After the Cold War purges, however, such alliances became rare as community-based social activist groups were treated as potential threats. Such an attitude, along with the predominant views of the AFL (which would merge with a weakened CIO in 1955 to become the AFL-CIO) led to significant backtracking. Organized labor felt less like a social movement and more like a trade association.

Ironically, the relative strength of organized labor persisted well into the 1960s and with it came an impact on the larger workforce. Many non-union companies, such as IBM, took steps to prevent unionization by keeping their wages and salaries nearly competitive with those of unionized facilities. Benefit packages for some of the larger non-union companies were often nearly competitive with unionized facilities in many parts of the country, excluding the South and Southwest, again as a means of discouraging workers from joining or forming labor unions. Companies would sometimes have alternative—nonbinding—grievance procedures, and supposedly "open door" policies suggesting that they were prepared to receive criticisms and suggestions.

When I first entered the workforce, in 1976, many of the non-union factories in Greater Boston had wages that were less than those of unionized facilities but not dramatically less in most cases. You could, however, count on a unionized facility to offer superior benefits. During the course of the 1980s, this changed, not only in

Boston but nationally due to increasing demands for concessions on unionized facilities (for example, Chrysler, followed by many other companies) and by the declining fear of unions by big corporations (specifically, the declining sense of unions as being capable of conducting the level of organizing that they once could).

IS A UNION A CLUB?

The contrast between the unionism of the 1930s and 1940s, and what existed in the 1960s through the 1980s could not have been starker. Contrary to the commitments made when the American Federation of Labor and Congress of Industrial Organizations merged in 1955, the union movement functioned like a business alignment. Certain unions permitted the exclusion of workers of color and women from their ranks and, during a time when social movements were addressing myriad issues including civil rights, foreign policy, and women's rights, the union movement closed ranks and acted as if these weren't important issues. While there were exceptions, the dominant practice of the movement advanced the perception that unions operated more like a club than as a vital social movement.

Despite the public stances unions often took in favor of different legislation, the inclusivity that characterized much of the union movement in the 1930s and 1940s had declined significantly by the mid to late 1950s. As a result, other movements, organizations, and in some cases lawyers, began to fill roles that unions might have played at an earlier point in history. The emergence of "wrongful termination" litigation in the late 1970s is one example of this. Rather than turning to unionization as a mechanism to oppose wrongful termination, non-union workers (professionals and nonprofessionals) looked for their day in court. For instance, the 1977 ruling in *Fortune v. National Cash Register Company*, a Massachusetts case involving the bad faith termination of a salesman in which he was deprived of a bonus, gave many people hope that the courts could become an effective mechanism for fighting wrongful termination. As it turned out, this didn't happen, but illusions concerning litigation addressed the absence of either large-scale unionization or the mechanism of labor courts.[4]

By the 1980s, the political Right, led by President Reagan, had successfully painted labor unions as a "special interest." Despite protests to the contrary, it became increasingly difficult for much of the public—even when they had latent sympathies toward unions— to see something broader than organizations looking out for the interests of their own members. Regardless of the hypocrisy of Reagan's attacks—given that the corporate forces that he represented were very "special" and self-interested—the label of "special interest group" was branded on the forehead of many a labor leader and the front door of many a union office.

ALTERNATIVES TO SPECIAL INTERESTS?

The union movement's responses to charges of being a "special interest" were largely defensive and truthfully ineffective. They ranged from a simple denial ("No, we aren't!") to efforts at good public relations to charity. Even today, the union movement frequently contributes significantly to charitable causes. In the aftermath of the Hurricane Katrina disaster, for instance, there was an outpouring of union assistance to the victims of the hurricane. Food, clothing, money, and forms of technical assistance were offered, yet this didn't undermine their image as a "special interest."

What too many union leaders failed to understand is that the "special interest" label didn't mean that the unions failed to care about anyone else in the narrow sense of the term. But rather that the unions had ceased speaking for anyone other than their members, and in some cases, only those in very specific industries. Or, to put it another way, large sections of the public had ceased looking to unions to speak for them, even on issues that were directly related to matters of economic injustice. While I've never subscribed to Reagan's criticism—or terminology—with regard to unions, the fact of the matter is that the practice of many unions has been something worthy of criticism.

There have always been unions and union-initiated programs

that have sought to break out of the old mold; consider these note-worthy examples:

- *West Coast dockworkers fight apartheid.* The International Long-shore and Warehouse Union (ILWU, aka the West Coast dock-workers union, was an early opponent of the apartheid system in South Africa (introduced in 1948). This shouldn't have been surprising given that the leadership of the ILWU, since its founding in 1936, had been progressive and global in their outlook. As a matter of self-preservation in a world of global commerce, dockworkers unions, internationally, have tended to be concerned about other dockworker unions globally. Nonetheless, the ILWU has gone beyond concerns specific to their industry, and the struggle against South African apartheid was one example. ILWU members, in the 1980s, refused to handle cargo coming in from South Africa, an act that put them at great risk. This was consistent with the stance they took in the 1930s when cargo was shipped from fascist nations.
- *Stamford, Connecticut, organizing project.* The national AFL-CIO began a series of initiatives in the late 1990s called "geographic organizing projects" that aimed to organize multiple workplaces/industries in the same locale. What made the Stamford project unique was the effort to turn worker organizing into both an alliance with community-based organizations as well as an effort toward economic development for the working class com-munity of that area. This effort included a commitment by the national AFL-CIO to provide funds toward housing develop-ment for the area, a commitment that addressed the very real problem of workers being unable to afford living in Stamford.[5]
- *Jobs with Justice.* Formed in the late 1980s largely as an effort to widen support for labor unions, the unique feature of JwJ was that it included unions and community-based organizations. Over time, JwJ involved itself in work that went beyond support-ing workers who were on strike or workers who were organizing

unions. They were involved in the anti–World Trade Organization demonstrations that took place in Seattle in 1999, and from
there became more involved in global worker rights issues.
Local chapters and coalitions of JwJ have taken up the cause
of the unemployed in many places, including efforts to organize
the unemployed in their fight for jobs and economic security.

- *Madison, Wisconsin, 2011.* An intriguing example of unions being
viewed as anything but a special interest can be found in the
Madison demonstrations against Republican governor Scott
Walker's draconian assault on working people. His attacks not
only included tax giveaways to the wealthy, but cutbacks on
benefits won by workers, and an attempt to deprive workers
of their full right to collective bargaining. Evidently, Walker
assumed that the unions would stand alone, but, contrary to his
expectations, there was a virtual uprising in Madison, with an
encampment along with demonstrations of tens of thousands
of workers, students, and their allies. This act of resistance
stunned the Republicans and was followed by a dynamic recall
election that won two out of six seats for Democrats in historically Republican districts. The fact that people responded so
favorably in defense of the unions spoke volumes about how the
Wisconsin union movement is perceived by much of the public.

- *AFL-CIO alliances with the National Domestic Workers Alliance
and the National Day Laborers Organizing Network.* Expanding
the fight for economic justice, these alliances are important
because they involve the unions supporting workers that have
either been excluded by the NLRA or have been otherwise
marginalized.

Each of these examples has its own unique features, but what's
striking is that each represents an effort to go beyond a more mun-
dane, so-called traditional union approach to economic justice. As
such, they reveal a fundamental point: there's nothing intrinsic in a
labor union that would make it narrow or blind to the issues facing

the broader public. However, leaving aside for a moment the barrage of right-wing propaganda against unions, there are practices that the union movement must take responsibility for. It's true that some unions have failed to organize new workers and have turned away potential allies. This must be acknowledged, but we must recognize that this reflects a certain practice of trade unionism that is itself a problem—if not *the* problem facing the union movement in this country.

"UNIONS AND CORPORATIONS ARE BOTH TOO BIG AND DON'T REALLY CARE ABOUT THE WORKER."

Whenever I hear someone talk about so-called "big labor" and "big business" as though they're equivalent, I start pulling my hair out. What, I ask, is "big labor" and how can anyone see labor and business comparable in size and strength?

If you look at the top fifty companies in the Fortune 500, you'll find market value ranging from $414 billion at the top (Exxon Mobil) to $51 billion at number fifty (Freeport-McMoRan Copper & Gold), as of March 2011.[1] By equity, the breakdown is as follows: Bank of America is number one with equity at $228 billion and WellPoint at number fifty with $23 billion.[2]

Now, it's incredibly difficult to compare a profit-making corporation with a not-for-profit one, but for the sake of argument, let's look at the following. The anti-union website, UnionFacts .com, reported that the national AFL-CIO has total assets of over $99 million with a total income of over $177 million in 2010.[3] According to this same website, the SEIU, one of the largest unions in the country with approximately 2 million members, has assets of more than $209 million with an income of more than $318 million.[4]

While for you and me, these numbers are astronomical, what's critical to understand is the difference in scale. SEIU's assets represent a shocking .05 percent of Exxon Mobil's market value![5] There's no need to go through the facts and figures for the other unions; the evidence is clear. We're not talking about even remotely comparable organizations.

This difference in scale causes a *power imbalance*, and the resources that big business can amass, whether for election campaigns or to oppose unionization efforts, are off the charts. But it's more than funds that are directly expended on a particular campaign. As opposed to unions, private corporations have a significant economic impact on the larger community, and decisions such as whether a company should invest in a particular locale creates a ripple effect that affects the community.

When it comes to labor there's at least one other aspect to this question of "big." In 1955, unions represented approximately 35 percent of the nonagricultural workforce. In 2011, that percentage was down to approximately 12 percent. The actual numbers today are around 16 million, out of a workforce of approximately 154 million.[6] Since 1980, unions have lost millions of members largely through so-called deindustrialization, while at the same time gained numbers in the public sector. In either case, they were unable to keep up with the growth of the workforce. If the unions had the same percentage as they did in 1955, union membership would be in the realm of 50 million members.

So, again, what does it mean to be called "big"? It actually becomes a misnomer and, in fact, an anachronistic expression when discussing today's union movement—"big" simply doesn't correspond with reality.

The power of corporate America has been growing significantly, and the rise of Rupert Murdoch and his various media outlets is only one example. Leaving aside the various newspapers under his control, the existence of Fox News and its many cable components offers the political right and their corporate allies an entire news network. Yet Fox is an extreme example of the forces that reshaped the United States, and in particular, the matter of media consolidation. Since 1995, according to Common Cause, the number of companies owning commercial TV stations declined by 40 percent. In cable, only three media giants (Comcast, Time Warner, and News Corporation) control all of cable news.[7]

In other words, what's unfolding isn't solely about the growth of right-wing, pro-corporate media, but the consolidation of corporate media as a whole and with it, the limitations on media democracy. This has meant that corporate voices, rather than a myriad of independent voices, have greater access to the public, irrespective of their particular political bent. An example of this is the disappearance of "labor reporters" from mainstream newspapers. Once a common position in most newspapers, this role has nearly vanished and, at best, been subsumed by the "business" section of the newspapers.

There's nothing comparable among unions to this trend toward increasing power. While there has been, over the last twenty years, an increase in the union mergers, these mergers haven't produced significant increases in power. In most cases, such mergers were the result of a declining (if not disappearing) union choosing to find a home in another more stable union. Many of these mergers make absolutely no strategic or industrial sense, and they may be based more on personal relationships or the specifics of a particular agreement between the two unions that seems to make the merger fit. But, for the most part, these aren't mergers that build power.

WHAT, THEN, IS ALL THIS ABOUT "BIG LABOR"?

Since the facts don't fit the anti-unionists' allegations, it's worth thinking about what *is* at stake when these charges are leveled at organized labor.

The charge of "big labor" was used to undermine organized labor's political influence largely from the period of FDR's New Deal through the 1960s. In that period, organized labor had a significant level of influence on government, though it never approached the impact of labor movements in Europe. Conservative political forces who hated the New Deal and concessions to working people tried to represent organized labor as a big ogre. Since the hand of big business isn't always evident in the political realm, at least not directly, it was fairly easy to suggest that both of these institutions were of equivalent size and strength.

But there's another source of this allegation. Many small business owners are scared of both big business and organized labor, although for very different reasons. Small business is scared of big business because they're worried about being wiped out. Think Walmart and big box chains versus a small hardware store. Walmart's size and relationship with contractors makes it possible to undercut most competitors, especially small businesses. At the same time, small business may come to identify with big business, particularly if a relationship can be built, through, for instance, subcontracting or getting around issues of taxes.

Small business is frequently petrified of labor unions. Because their profit margin is often slim and their workforces small, small business owners are habitually fearful that unions will take them under and that they'll lose control of their operation.

This challenge of small business is one that I encountered in my early days as a union organizer when I was involved with organizing and representing small child-care facilities. While these were nonprofits, the psyche of small business ownership was very much in line with the thinking of the leaders of these institutions. Despite an organizing strategy that suggested to these nonprofits that the union was interested in working together to improve the financing of child-care facilities and the conditions of the child-care workers, many directors were prepared to go to war with the union. While at first glance this seemed irrational, on further examination it becomes clear that this was about power and a deep fear that organized workers would somehow dethrone these agency heads. In some cases, no amount of discussion could convince them otherwise. Therefore, while it was in their immediate *and* long-term economic interests to collaborate with the union to improve the economic vitality of the institution, the fear of a loss of control overwhelmed them.

This profound fear operates among many small business own-ers. As a result, they're open to being influenced by propaganda that suggests there are twin evils in the economy: "big labor" and "big business," not to mention certain governmental bodies. A segment of the political right plays on these fears and discourages any sense that small business and organized labor can, on many things, work together and represent a common front against the megacorpora-tions that have come to dominate the economy.

The facts clearly disprove the charge of "big labor" demonstrat-ing that it's yet another myth that seeks to defame unions, pure and simple and, in effect, let big business off the hook. Big business, like our friends at Exxon Mobil, are in control of the commanding heights of the economy rather than the organizations of workers—unions—that simply cannot compare with these corporations in terms of size, assets, or affect the economy.

"LET'S FACE IT, IN A GLOBALIZED WORLD, UNIONS ARE POWERLESS."

> The combined dynamics of capital mobility, the transnational
> fragmentation of production, and neoliberal policies contribute
> to what has been termed the "race to the bottom," . . . of labor
> standards in the global economy where workers are left without
> an effective regulatory framework to protect and advance labor
> rights.[1]
>
> —*Mark P. Thomas*

Although many people act as if shifting sites of production (for example, plant closings) are something new, that's far from true. Throughout the capitalist world, such occurrences are historically typical. In the United States, for instance, we can look to the shift of the textile and garment industry from the Northeast to the South. As a child and later as a teenager, I remember driving along Route 95 in Rhode Island, and Route 6 (and later the parallel Route 195) from Providence to Cape Cod. Along the way, I'd see the shells of factories that had been abandoned years before, leaving towns such as Providence, Fall River, and New Bedford a shadow of their one-time glory.

By the mid-to-late 1970s, dramatic changes were unfolding in the global economy. In response to economic stagnation, new policies were instituted to spark economic growth, albeit at the expense of working people. Combined with developments in technology, the world of work evolved dramatically and included the movement of production sites, downsizing, and, in some cases, the outright closings of facilities. As opposed to the experience of the Northeast, in which only one industry was affected, what came to be known as *deindustrialization* had an impact on the North, Midwest, West Coast, and, much later, the Southeast and Southwest, which initially benefited from deindustrialization.

Both the reality and the threat of shifting production had a dramatic impact on working people and their organizations. As my late friend Dr. Bennett Harrison used to say, deindustrialization represented a "credible threat" aimed at the heads of working people. Simply put, he meant that the employer class could point to plant closings and say that unless workers were prepared to take concessions, or unless workers refused to organize or join a union, the employer would shut down the facility and move it elsewhere, like to Ciudad Juárez, Mexico. Whether the company could or would do this was inconsequential. The question was whether the workers and the neighboring communities *believed* that it might happen.

Shifting production through, for example, off-shoring was originally situated within manufacturing, but that changed in the 1990s as a result of the electronics revolution. We started to see the "off-shoring" of white-collar jobs, which was a jolt for most workers.[2] These dramatic changes sent shockwaves throughout the union movement and continue to reverberate. In fact, the union movement hasn't developed a clear and consistent response to these changes. However, there are emerging trends worth examining.

A HISTORICAL NOTE . . . THOUGH NOT A TANGENT

At times when the capitalist economy has shifted, worker organizations have been thrown into disarray. By "shifting," I'm not referring to the boom-and-bust cycles of capitalism, but rather the more dramatic changes in the economy. For instance, the creation of factories and the move away from domestic work and small-scale skilled labor undermined the old guilds and altered the relationship of women to work outside of the home. The creation of mass production industries in the early part of the twentieth century, for instance, auto and steel, couldn't be addressed by most of the largely skilled trade unions within the American Federation of Labor. Despite various experiments, the efforts to organize mass production industries using the framework of the skilled trades failed.[3] At each moment of disarray or crisis, unions were decried by the mainstream media as irrelevant, outmoded, or archaic. Unions, along with other forms of worker organizations, reemerged looking quite different. But in each case, their form of organization had to correspond, at some level, to the nature of the industry in which they were operating. For that reason, throughout the history of unions, one can see transitions in forms of organization as industries shift and reshape themselves.

THE ISSUE OF POWER

Changes in production—part of the "world of work"—are motivated by an assortment of concerns. For instance, new technology can increase productivity through output, but it'd be wrong to assume that it's developed for that reason alone. Changes in production are often inspired by efforts on the part of the employer class to weaken the relative power of workers. That power may derive from their knowledge of the production process or that which they exert through force of sheer numbers. In either case, power is at stake when the production process evolves, irrespective of the rhetoric used at the time.

An example of this phenomenon comes from the 1980s when, partly inspired by economic developments in Japan, US employers began using the terminology of "quality" and later "partnership" when they were introducing changes in the workplace. Forms of "quality" organization were aimed at allegedly giving workers a voice in the production process. These were seductive mechanisms that served to obtain from the workers greater levels of information about how work was actually conducted. With this knowledge, employers redesigned workplaces and, in most cases, eliminated workers as part of the process.

While one can argue that this was all part of a process of improving work, what it did, in effect, was to strengthen the hand of the employer and obtained information and knowledge from workers with almost nothing in return. Yet workers were often so enticed by the fact that their opinions were being sought—often for the first times in their work lives—that they would cooperate, at least until it became clear that the objectives of the employers were frequently less than noble. In some cases, the union leaders themselves would be seduced by the *apparent* interest of the employer in a different sort of relationship with the union. This relationship frequently came at the cost of concessions to management and worse, the expectation that the union leaders would think with a pro-management bias rather than their starting point being the interests of the workers.

The point here is that the global economic changes we've witnessed over the last forty years aren't the natural evolution of the economy but are the result of political decisions by governmental bodies, and the introduction of technologies that strive to cut costs at the expense of workers. By weakening the power of workers, their ability to organize and to demand their rights and living standard improvements has become that much more difficult, prompting pro-business media outlets to declare the death of organized labor.

EXPERIMENTS, RESISTANCE, AND CHALLENGES

One of the first things to understand is that not all businesses can "run," that is, shut down and leave town. Some, like governmental bodies, by their very definition, must stay put; however, this doesn't stop them from subcontracting some of their work. In the private sector, there are companies that must stay close to their domestic market(s). There are also sectors of the economy like the logistics, or transportation, industry that are directly tied to the global market but need domestic linkages to function. Therefore, while new technologies and the reduction of workers in various industries mean that workplaces don't resemble 1946, new vulnerabilities become pressure points for workers in their fights for dignity. Retired

University of California-Riverside professor Edna Bonacich and writer Khaleelah Hardie noted this in a thought-provoking article concerning Walmart. They wrote:

> Some [weaknesses and vulnerabilities in production and distribution] are clearly evident, including extended supply chains and networks which can potentially be cut; JIT [Just In Time] delivery, whose interruption can be devastating; nodes, like ports and airports . . . links to the global workforce . . . branding of the retailers, who are then vulnerable to increasing public exposure and criticism; and the fact that the giant retailers . . . deal directly with consumers, who are also workers and citizens. The international trade community is aware of some of these vulnerabilities . . . framing the danger as the threat of a terrorist attack, rather than labor disruption.[4]

Bonacich and Hardie speak to the fact that the union movement must think very differently about the strategies that it pursues and not, as it were, fighting the "last war." New conditions necessitate new strategies and forms of organization, not to mention, new tactics. An interesting example of a successful struggle against a transnational corporation that brought together key elements of a twenty-first-century approach was conducted by the ILWU against the Rio Tinto corporation and its mining facilities in Boron, California. The struggle is summarized in an insightful article by veteran labor activist and ILWU organizing director Peter Olney.[5] In this struggle, Rio Tinto was attempting to crush the union and, essentially, hoping to force the workers into a strike they couldn't win. When it was unable to do so, the corporation carried out a lockout (blocking the workers from going to work). Olney summarizes key elements from the workers' campaign, including the following:

- *Research.* Truly understanding the nature and objectives of Rio Tinto, but also their relative strengths and weakness. This also included understanding the relative strengths and weaknesses of the union.

- *Contract campaign.* A "contract campaign" refers to a method of carrying out a struggle where the workers mobilize, seek allies, and carry out various forms of pressure on the employer. Contract campaigns, which became popular in the 1990s after being largely abandoned in the aftermath of the Cold War labor purges of the 1940s, are contrasted with more passive forms of activity that unions conducted for so long (e.g., low-level involvement by members; discussions at the bargaining table about which the members know little; an overreliance on strikes as a form of pressure). In this case, Olney notes the importance of the following:
  - Message: The union needed a clear message about what it was fighting and the nature of the battle (in this case, a David versus Goliath struggle).
  - Money: The union needed to build up its reserves so that if/ when Rio Tinto forced them out, the members would be able to survive financially.
  - Mobilization: The union needed to be prepared to fight, engaging its members in this and winning over key allies.

The combination of these activities, plus the courage of the membership under adverse conditions, laid the foundation for victory. In addition to these factors, the ILWU understood that the company would be under pressure because of the loss of the skilled and semi-skilled workers from their regular workforce. Thus, even though the company employed scabs during the lockout, the scabs weren't a quality workforce, thereby hurting the company.

The Rio Tinto struggle wasn't a singular anomaly. On the East Coast, a separate union of dockworkers—a local union of the International Longshoremen's Association—engaged in a nearly two-year campaign to win the freedom of five of its members who had been set up when the government of South Carolina, in collaboration with an employer, attempted to crush the local union. The case became internationally known as the Charleston 5 Case, and it was one I was associated with.[6]

As with the Rio Tinto campaign, unorthodox approaches were needed to fight for the freedom of the five dockworkers accused of conspiracy to incite to riot and inciting to riot. Traditional union approaches would probably have involved a reliance on lawyers and perhaps a letter-writing campaign to the governor of South Carolina. Instead, the campaign moved from being limited to Charleston to what was, in effect, an international campaign that included the following:

- *Defense committees around the United States.* Committees to support the workers were formed in many cities by union members and their allies to raise funds and build publicity for the campaign. The aim was to build a national presence that would pressure the state of South Carolina.
- *Dockworker unions around the world were enlisted.* Dockworker unions understood that the attack on the Charleston dockworkers wouldn't end with Charleston but would be something that other dockworkers would face. These unions were prepared to put intense pressure on the shipping line to back off.
- *A large national demonstration in Columbia, South Carolina.* South Carolina's largest labor demonstration since the 1930s was held in the state capitol to protest the case, receiving national publicity in the mainstream media.
- *An excellent legal team was enlisted to represent the workers.* They built a strong case.
- *Use of the media.* The defense campaign utilized different media outlets to get across its message about the racial and class dynamics of this struggle.
- *Isolating the attorney general.* South Carolina's attorney general was the architect of the attack on the dockworkers, so it was critical that he be isolated. By the end of the case, he had become a pariah in the state.

- *Having a solid core for the fight.* Without the leadership of the president of the dockworkers union of Charleston (Kenneth Riley), the support of the members of his local union (ILA Local 1422) and a national core of labor union staff, volunteers, and attorneys, this fight would have gone nowhere.

In the examples of both Rio Tinto and Charleston 5, the use of the media and garnering public support were crucial to the successes of the campaigns.[7] Not surprisingly, unions have found that winning public support for a struggle can be decisive in determining whether there is a victory, regardless of whether that struggle is a domestic or global fight.[8] That public support may be evidenced in various ways, but it inevitably changes the condition of the battle.

Also in response to the globalization of business, many unions have created "International Framework Agreements" that are established among international alliances of unions in the same economic sector—called "global union federations"—and specific transnational corporations. These are aimed primarily at gaining the agreement of a transnational corporation to permit full labor rights for the workers of that company. These IFAs are distinguished from the unilaterally announced "codes of conduct" that many corporations have undertaken where there is, by definition, no union involvement. Theoretically, IFAs permit unions to freely operate and conduct bargaining.[9] These aren't, however, global collective bargaining agreements, and, as such, their success ultimately depends on three factors: the relative strength of the unions that compose the global union federations, their respective abilities to operate in their homelands, and the level of pressure on the transnational corporations to comply.

Unions are increasingly collaborating across borders. While there is a historical precedent for this, today's collaboration has been driven less by ideology and more by the practical realities of the global economic shift.[10] This has both an upside and downside, because the fact remains that cooperation driven by practical matters alone often leads to a short-sighted approach with regard to building international cooperation rather than understanding the long-term necessity for unity. That said, global cooperation in either case involves a series of challenges that range from different languages and cultures to the relative strength of different unions to often vastly different approaches to collective bargaining.

A wealthy businessman once told me, with a complete absence of emotion, that when workers in plants that he owns seek to organize, he simply shuts down the plant. He didn't seem to feel that modus operandi was callous or insulting, not to mention illegal, but rather a simple statement of fact. That he could shut down his plants without remorse speaks volumes to the extent of the labor laws of the United States, the weakening of unions, the developments in the global economy, and the "looking out for number one philosophy" so fundamental to neoliberalism. For these reasons, unions have developed new approaches toward building power, a few of which have been mentioned. At its core, however, unions—domestically and globally—need to convince a broader slice of the population that the cause of economic justice is *their* cause, and not just the cause of those who belong to unions.

"WHERE DO UNIONS STAND ON IMMIGRANTS—YOU EITHER IGNORE THEM OR YOU IGNORE THE REST OF US?"

Immigration has been one of the most difficult issues that organized labor has faced in its existence. It overlaps with matters of race but has its own identity, which makes it even more complicated. So, let's take a quick glimpse of the issue of immigration historically and then what it has meant—and means today—for unions.

THE SETTING

Immigration in the United States has always been shaped by one fundamental issue: this country was founded as a home for settlers moving to North America from Europe. There was no attempt to forge a nation-state with the indigenous (Native American) population or, at least until 1865 (at the earliest), with the imported African slaves. In fact, the dominant—though not exclusive—conception of the founders was of a European colony and, eventually, a Euro-American state.

As discussed earlier, the ruling elite in the thirteen North American colonies had a great deal of trouble controlling the laboring classes of the colonies. Race became a means of accomplishing

three things: justifying the removal (and extermination if necessary) of Native Americans, the enslavement for life of Africans, and
social control over the entire laboring population.

This process of creating a category known as "white" invited two
critical questions: who was "white" and how did you know? These
questions were answered differently at different moments in history. For this reason, immigration policy, after the formation of the
United States, changed over time, and was often met with stiff internal resistance. As a group, the English, Scots, French, German,
and Swedes who were here by the early 1800s weren't particularly
welcoming to other European populations. Among the most well-
known victims of anti-immigrant fervor were the Irish. While the
Irish were clearly European, they came from a British colony and
were looked down upon by the British, who considered them an
inferior "race." For other European immigrants, much the same
fate awaited them with varying degrees of violent resistance to their
presence. But if they weren't "white," that put them into a social and
political twilight zone. They couldn't be enslaved, but they could be
subordinated in an implicit socioeconomic hierarchy to the largely
Protestant immigrants who preceded them, and they could be subject to various forms of discrimination. Over time, however, these
groups came to be integrated into the larger "white" population, and
their ethnic identities became less a badge of identification. Rather,
the critical distinction was that they weren't African American, Native American, Mexican American, or Asian American populations.[1]

Immigration to the United States has favored Europe from the
beginning, and, despite the initial and frequent hostility received
by many of these immigrants, Europeans were absorbed into the
larger so-called white majority. Even though immigration laws have
changed over time, most especially in the mid-1960s, the conditions under which European immigrants operated have always been
distinct from those encountered by immigrants of color, that is,
Asians, Africans, Caribbeans, and Latin Americans. Interestingly,
this is true with respect to the treatment of both undocumented and
documented immigrants.

WHY DO THEY COME HERE?

Discussions of immigration in the mainstream media tend to assume that all people migrate to the United States for essentially the same reason and are driven by the same causes. Poverty in Ireland, along with the potato famine (a result of British colonialism), resulted in the exodus of at least a million Irish. Deep-seated poverty in southern Italy led to a major migration. Virulent anti-Semitism in Eastern Europe encouraged approximately 2.5 million Jews to leave their homes and travel to the United States. All the while, of course, US industry was looking for more labor power.

Immigration patterns from countries of origin outside of Europe were driven by some similar and some very different sources, a fact which should, theoretically, affect national policy but is regularly ignored even by most unions. Following 1965, immigrants increasingly came from war-torn regions or places where the United States was involved economically or politically. Migration from Indochina in the aftermath of the wars in Vietnam, Laos, and Cambodia is one example. Another example is migration from Latin America, particularly Central America, in the 1980s from countries that had long been dominated by US economic interests and were often in the midst of civil wars in which the United States played a direct role (in supporting repressive governments). Migration from Latin America was also deeply affected by trade agreements, such as NAFTA (where migration from Mexico increased approximately 60 percent), and their economic impact on the domestic industries of Latin American and Caribbean nations.

Compounding this is the fact that US economic interests sought cheap and vulnerable labor power. In response to the restructuring of the global economy, domestic industries themselves restructured and targeted specific populations of workers considered vulnerable. At times, this led to something equivalent to an ethnic cleansing of industries and the replacement of the workforce by workers who were assumed to be more malleable.

It's important to keep in mind that various economic "niches" change over time with respect to their race/ethnicity. This is driven by economic and political forces that see in a new population one that can be exploited to benefit employers. In that sense, it is rare indeed to find a particular occupation that has remained "in the hands" of a particular ethnic group for an indefinite period since employers are always looking for a new and vulnerable population.

UNIONS RESPOND . . . OR REACT?

Going back to the nineteenth century, European immigrants were often the backbone of the white side of organized labor. One need only remember the immigrant (largely Jewish) women in New York who transformed protest into unionization in the garment industry. But this was true in other sectors. John Sayles dramatized this phenomenon in his excellent historically based film *Matewan*, which concerns West Virginia miners in the early 1920s. The European immigrant workers in his film had not "become white" yet and were still an alienated group in a strange land coexisting with nonimmigrant whites and with African American workers.

Yet, at the same time, organized labor in the United States was ambivalent about immigration. In addition, there were diametrically opposed approaches when it came to immigration from Europe versus immigration from Asia. Overwhelmingly organized (white) labor favored Asian *exclusion* and, in many cases, *outright deportation*. Asian labor on the West Coast was presented as a threat to white labor, and this threat was *racialized*. In a pattern that would become all too familiar, it wasn't just that Asian labor was alleged to have been competing with white labor, but the proponents of Asian exclusion developed an entire set of propositions regarding Asians and the alleged danger they represented to white America.[2] Another term for this is "demonization," and the particular terminology at the time was the description of Asians as the "yellow peril." This contrasted with the treatment of European immigrants who, after being victims of discrimination and harassment, were able to find a niche in the economy within which they could operate and in many cases grow.

Labor in the United States was divided over this question of immigration. Think about the inclusion/exclusion dichotomy we discussed elsewhere. With regard to immigration, essentially three general patterns emerged over time:

- *Exclusion.* This could be outright exclusion, such as the Knights of Labor barring Chinese labor, or a subtler or de facto exclusion (a pattern in evidence in the building trades unions for most of the twentieth century).
- *Modified inclusion.* This applied almost entirely to European immigrants, but meant that portions of a union might open up to a particular immigrant group. For instance, the same union might have local unions dominated by one or another European ethnic group. In other cases, a particular trade or craft would be dominated by a particular European immigrant population.
- *Inclusion.* The Industrial Workers of the World were among the most consistent on this, but there were other unions such as the Mine, Mill, and Smelters Union and the Food, Tobacco, Agricultural and Allied Workers (CIO). These were unions that were open to migrant workers and actively seeking to organize them.

In times of economic distress, anti-immigrant fervor would strengthen and become the dominant feature within the union movement. Yet, during the twentieth century (and certainly in these early years of the twenty-first century), this fervor hasn't been turned against European immigrant populations. While it is demonstrably the case that various European immigrant groups have faced discrimination and prejudice, none have been subject to the scapegoating, harassment, and immigrant hunting that Asian, Caribbean, and Latino immigrants (and, in some cases, African immigrants) have. One of the most notorious events in US history was the massive expulsion of hundreds of thousands of Chicano and Mexicano residents—many documented US citizens—during the Great Depression of the 1930s.[3] This transpired because of the alleged threat of Mexican labor to US citizens, yet this expulsion or ethnic cleansing did nothing to address the issue of unemployment faced by millions of people in the country at that time.

The racial discrepancy in immigration is rarely discussed in the mainstream media but has been evident for years, both in terms of who is targeted for deportation and the nature of demonization. Consider the fact that the Russian mafia, which emerged after the Cold War, is rarely used as a poster for Russian immigrants. Contrast that with the notorious Salvadoran gang MS-13 and the manner in which Salvadoran (and other Latino youth) are often assumed to be part of such groupings. Or, for that matter, the demonization of Nigerians and the assumption that Nigerians are all tied in with gangs and Internet scams.

WHAT IS THE CHALLENGE FOR THE UNIONS?

In the face of immigration—documented and undocumented—much of the union movement rushed to support employer sanctions and other such controls in the 1980s.[4] Some even went further and supported steps such as the militarization of the border and the creation of the so-called fence aimed at stopping immigrants. One might wonder: Is this *all* about racism and xenophobia?

The answer is no—it's certainly influenced by racism and xenophobia, but it's far more complicated. Racism most clearly shows its face when there's a failure to acknowledge the differential in treatment between European and non-European immigrants (currently and historically) and particularly the demonization of immigrants of color. What's been transpiring for the unions is particularly driven by the competition for jobs, especially as the economy restructures and there are no longer any safe spaces.

Unions observe that employers bring in immigrants—documented and undocumented—with the intent of removing current workers and reducing costs. Some unions then conclude that if sanctions are imposed on the employers (assuming the employer is caught) for using undocumented labor this will discourage the importation of such workers. As for legal immigrants, some suggest that there be a moratorium on all immigration.

Let's first look at the undocumented side of this equation. Many unions have concluded that sanctioning employers simply doesn't work. In fact, what happens is that the immigrant worker is criminalized, meaning that an employer can use the undocumented worker, but as soon as said worker gets out of line (for instance, by supporting a union), the employer will call Immigration and Customs Enforcement (ICE) to have that worker removed. The employer isn't penalized and may simply hire another vulnerable worker.

The larger problem is that competition among companies drives employers to hire workers at cheaper and cheaper costs. Inevitably, employers will take their chances and seek whatever vulnerable workforce they can.

Employer sanctions do not decrease the competition for jobs, but neither will a moratorium on all immigration. As long as there are trade agreements such as NAFTA and US military intervention in the internal affairs of other countries, dispossessed populations will seek a better life and will travel to the sites of economies with which they have a historical relationship. This is remarkably different from the migration to the United States in the early part of the twentieth century. If there's a moratorium on immigration, then there will be a lot of undocumented immigration. If the United States doesn't take responsibility for the conditions that it has often brought about overseas, people will travel here seeking a better life, giving truth to the slogan of the immigrant rights movement in Britain, "We are here because you were there."

Many unions began concluding at least a piece of this beginning in the early 1990s, thus leading to a different take on immigration within much of organized labor. As a result of both a growing awareness of the impact of immigration on the workforce plus the activism of the immigrant rights movement (and their allies in organized labor), the AFL-CIO and increasing segments of organized labor as a whole began to see, much as the old IWW did, that once workers are here, they need to be organized. When African American workers began migrating from the South during World War I, they were sought after by corporations looking for cheap labor.[5] These corporations cared for African Americans only as a vulnerable population to exploit. White unions largely refused to organize these workers and the African Americans tended to see the unions as an enemy rather than a potential friend. It was only with a different approach by white organized labor—an inclusive approach undertaken by certain sections of white organized labor—that something very dramatic happened: the labor upsurge of the 1930s and the formation of the CIO.

To be clear, the awakening among many unions hasn't necessarily been driven by an ideological revelation. In most cases the restructuring of their respective industries and the demographic changes that have taken place have necessitated a new approach, although with new approaches arise complications. The building trades/construction industry, for instance, was 41.4 percent unionized in 1966; 31.6 percent in 1979; 22 percent in 1989; and 13.1 percent in 2010.[6] While this transformation in union density has been underway, immigrant workers have been brought in by non-union contractors to reduce the overall wage and benefits of construction workers. The non-union contractors, with their underpaid immigrant workforces, have been increasingly squeezing the unionized contractors. The building trades unions—at least some of them—have been forced to address this through organizing many of these immigrant—documented and undocumented—workers. It's become a situation of "organize or die."

Yet for the unions, and especially those committed to organizing immigrant workers, there are delicate questions about nonimmigrant labor, and the tensions are often quite evident in different unions. Once I was asked to speak with leaders and staff from one building trades union about race and immigration, and it became clear early on that many of the African American workers felt that they were being ignored by the union's leadership in favor of the Latino immigrant workers. At the same time, many of the Latino workers felt that the African Americans weren't being good allies.

Situations such as this one can't be resolved by moral platitudes or expressions of good intentions. The tensions reflected in that meeting were the result of a history that has often meant that African Americans are placed in subservient roles. But that history doesn't stop there; it's also a history of some unions attempting to preserve their own ethno-organizational culture at the same time that the workforce and demographics are shifting. The reality is that neither factor can be ignored. Precisely for that reason, the approach taken by the United Food and Commercial Workers in organizing workers at the Smithfield plant in Tar Heel, North Carolina, was so significant. From the beginning, the leadership of the campaign placed a premium on building unity between the African American, white, and Latino immigrant workforce. They recognized the tensions that existed and did not try to avoid them but instead addressed them. The victory in this campaign is a tribute to this approach.

As in previous eras, a struggle has been underway for the soul of organized labor, in this case, over the question of immigration. Movements among immigrants have been pressing organized labor to favor its "inclusionist" side and embrace the demographic changes underway. Formations, such as the newly created Excluded Workers Congress, are attempting to reach out to immigrant and nonimmigrant worker groups that have been frequently ignored by organized labor and build them as a cohesive force.[7] The hope is that a real partnership can be constructed with organized labor.

To the original question, then, the answer seems to be that within organized labor there remain significant elements of the old view that excludes immigrants, particularly undocumented immigrants, in the name of preserving the living standard of nonimmigrant workers. At the same time, there's a segment of organized labor that has concluded that the only way to preserve *and raise* the living standard of the worker is to organize them into unions—and thereby build strength—irrespective of whether they're immigrant or nonimmigrant.[8]

"IF UNIONS ARE SO GOOD, WHY AREN'T THEY GROWING?"

All too often I find myself challenged by someone who asks me pointedly why unions aren't growing, and I'm reminded of the memorable words from the play *Jesus Christ Superstar* when King Herod says to Jesus, "Prove to me that you're divine. Change my water into wine."

EMPLOYER POWER CORRUPTS ABSOLUTELY

It's important to reiterate that one must recognize the impact of employer power, both the direct impact but also the indirect impact at the level of perception.

The employer's ability to terminate a worker for organizing a union (or organizing anything, as a matter of fact) has a chilling effect on worker morale. The fact that someone has the right to organize means little if in reality it takes months, if not years, to reinstate them from an illegal termination; assuming, of course, they win their case. That mere fact is something that workers can look at and conclude that it is not worth the trouble and potential danger to organize a union.[1]

A second factor that affects the ability of unions to grow is the response of employers when the union wins an election. I've had firsthand experiences with this and can attest that it can turn ugly. If it wishes to keep resisting the fact that the workers chose a union or formed a union, the employer can engage in delaying tactics to put off bargaining. Employers know that there is a one-year period to negotiate a first contract (collective bargaining agreement), at which time there can be what is called a "decertification election," where the workers can vote to dump the union. Therefore, if employers can utilize delaying tactics and make the entire process seem worthless, they attempt to undermine morale and lead the workers to throw up their hands in despair.

It's helpful to understand the process. After union elections, it's common for many workers who were engaged in the campaign to resign. This often results from fatigue or anger, but the bottom line is that a union can lose some of its core constituency. When the core is lost or weakened, it becomes that much more difficult for the union to survive. In the face of discouraging news from the bargaining table, things can collapse.

The employer has the upper hand in two significant ways. First, they can actively oppose unionization through methods such as captive audience meetings, threats to move the facility, implied threats, disciplinary actions, and terminations. While these may be illegal, the employer counts on the fact that it'll take years for a worker to fight such a case and that the worker will probably give up. Second, when the union attempts to engage in negotiations, the employer can drag them out. Keep in mind that the employer doesn't have to agree to anything; it simply has to "bargain in good faith."

Therefore, employer resistance is directly tied to the problem of the NLRA. In addition to the impact of the Taft-Hartley amendments to the NLRA in 1947, which put shackles on unions, there are insufficient penalties for employer interference in what should be a worker's right to choose representation. This is what many activists and scholars have found astonishing over the years. Employers can brazenly break the law only to be told that they have to post a notice saying they'll never break the law again, or, in the case of a termination, they *may* be compelled to pay back wages and benefits. In most other contractual situations, such activities would result in significant financial damages being awarded.

We start with employer power because it's both the most obvious, but it's also another example of the inconsistencies in our democracy. As we noted earlier, when workers enter the workplace they're entering what is, in effect, an authoritarian environment. The absence of "freedom of association," and in this case the absence of the full right to free and fair elections to choose a bargaining representative absent outside repression, clearly demonstrates the power imbalance discussed throughout this book.

JOB LOSS

One direct reason for the decline of unions has been the loss of membership, but this must be understood with discernment. The absolute number of union members hit a high of about 20 million in 1980, but as a percentage of the workforce, it was roughly 23 percent—a 9 percent decline from 32.5 percent density (in 1953). In either case, within three years of 1980, roughly 3 million workers were no longer union members.[2]

This job loss occurred during the infamous recession of the first years of the Reagan administration. It was a time of shaking out, so to speak, and rampant deindustrialization. It was also a key moment during which workers were expected—by businesses—to accept employers' concession demands to keep their facilities operating. The job loss was overwhelmingly in manufacturing. As I'll discuss later, the larger problem was that the unions weren't keeping pace with the growth of the workforce. That said, this dramatic loss of workers had a devastating impact on the landscape of the union movement. Among other things, many of the younger workers were eliminated; those who remained were often looking over their shoulders waiting for the next shoe to drop. This tense climate didn't create a particularly good atmosphere for growth.

Employers used this to their advantage and would often tell workers who were considering joining or forming a union that the unions hadn't been able to stop the job loss, therefore there was no value to them. This is a disingenuous argument, however, since a union is a bargaining instrument for workers and doesn't control the production process and can't stop the plant closings. This, however, doesn't dissuade a sense of despair among many workers.[3] To use a military analogy, in the face of an enemy's offensive, if a major front collapses, other fronts can stumble.

KEEPING PACE

What's fascinating about the growth challenge for unions is that they continued to grow until 1980. At the same time, as a percentage of the workforce, unions declined. So, they weren't keeping pace with the growth of the workforce. The question, then, is, Why not?

There are many reasons,[4] but let me suggest a few summary points. Be aware that these points are highly critical of traditional unionism and in no way try to hide from public view what unions failed to do.

The loss of the left wing of labor. At different points, I've raised my criticisms and concerns regarding the purges of the late 1940s that led to the loss of much of the left wing of organized labor. While many of the expelled unions from the CIO continued to exist, they declined in strength and were often raided by other CIO unions.

In many respects, the more radical unions of the CIO represented the soul of the new (1930s) union movement. They tended to be innovative and reached out to sectors of the workforce previously ignored. They were audacious and prepared to experiment with different pressure tactics on employers. As mentioned earlier, they also helped turn the cause of organized labor into *a popular cause.*

It's significant, then, to contrast the approach the CIO took toward attempting to organize the American South (1946–1951) with what they did only a few years earlier when they first emerged. After World War II, when the CIO announced "Operation Dixie," they went out of their way to exclude the political Left. What's more, they chose to ignore the developing Black Freedom Movement. The CIO treated its organizing of the South (and initially this was of the textile industry) as something that could be done in isolation from the major issues facing the South, especially the struggle against Jim

Crow segregation. Therefore, rather than the CIO unions and later the AFL-CIO unions being integral to the struggle for black freedom, they were often marginal. In some cases, some unions were actually opponents.

This was one ramification of the expulsion of the Left and the attempt to find legitimacy and respectability through such a Faustian bargain with business and the pro–Cold War elements of government.

Complacency. The movement lost its sense of urgency. During the 1950s and 1960s, AFL-CIO President George Meany wasn't worried about the declining strength of organized labor in part because that decline was inconsistent and slow (plus he came from a union—the United Association of Plumbers and Steamfitters of the United States and Canada—that had itself been very exclusive when it came to membership). There was an expectation that organized labor might drop a few percentage points, but there remained an assumption that it'd remain a significant player nevertheless.

It was also true that in the North, Midwest, and on the West Coast, there were no significant efforts to annihilate organized labor. This doesn't mean there weren't battles—there were—but there wasn't a sense in the North, Midwest, and West Coast that business was attempting to eliminate organized labor altogether. In the South and Southwest, however, it was different, with a deeply hostile attitude toward labor. Though even with that hostility, there was still an active union movement. As a result, there was a sense among many leaders that unions were here to stay.

One indication of complacency was the failure of unions to dedicate significant resources to member education and new organizing. For many unions organizing became an afterthought and wasn't considered the cutting edge of trade unionism. Instead, the unions settled on what's known as "industrial jurisprudence," i.e., grievances and arbitrations, and at best used collective bargaining negotiations as a means to secure jurisdiction over new facilities when they opened. While unions, as institutions, continued to grow until about 1980, the growth rate was insufficient and the approach toward organizing was largely ad hoc, with certain rare exceptions.

Growth of new sectors with which traditional labor was unfamiliar. This actually has a double meaning—the growth of new demographic groups and the growth of new sectors of the economy. With regard to demographic groups, from the 1960s to the 1970s, the biggest single change in the workforce was the increase in the number of women employees. As the women's movement and changes in the economy converged, women increasingly worked outside of the house. Organized labor was slow to respond to this, and in some cases, such as in the building trades, was resistant to the increasing presence of women. Some unions welcomed women and, as a result, there were increases in women in staff and leadership, but the unions weren't ahead of the curve.

There were other demographic changes. People of color, as a result of their respective freedom and justice movements, were entering sectors of the economy from which many had been excluded, such as the public sector. In that regard, they were looking for support from the unions, but it was inconsistent. One of the biggest challenges was the desegregation of workplaces, a challenge that many union leaders avoided. This could mean anything from failing to open their ranks, as with the building trades, to failure to open up greater opportunities within the industry to more skilled occupations, as with textile and steel.

The other aspect concerned sectors of the economy. As the 1950s evolved into the 1960s, workplace automation began eliminating jobs. At the same time, the growth of new jobs was largely untouched by unions. Banks were essentially absent any unions. There was an explosive growth in retail, only some of which was unionized. Over time, technology-producing jobs, particularly in electronics, expanded. New forms of communications were developed, and while unions were active in television, radio, and film, as the technologies changed, unions didn't respond quickly. In addition, the US economy witnessed the entrance of what came to be known as "transplants." These are industries, such as foreign autos, that while unionized in other parts of the world, fought unionization efforts in the United States tooth and nail.

In each of these cases, unions were either unable to develop appropriate strategies or were slow to develop them. In certain situations, the threat wasn't recognized; a development may have looked temporary or insignificant. In other cases, there was a recognition that in order to address a threat, something dramatic would need to change in the way the union operated, and such a change was too unsettling for many leaders to contemplate.

The challenge of technology and changes in the production process. The renaissance of organized labor in the United States in the 1930s took place in the context of the mass production industries. Gargantuan facilities spotted the countryside, with thousands of workers often employed in individual factories and shipyards. In the 1970s, the shipyard in which I worked employed several thousand workers at its height. Yet, with the introduction of new technologies, the production process shifted and "downsizing" began. In some cases, downsizing simply meant cost-cutting; but in other cases, such as that of the steel industry, it meant a decrease in workers with the increase in technology or getting out of the production of steel entirely.

Accompanying new technologies and new production processes were aggressive anti-union employers. Open-pit mining in the West, for instance, is largely non-union and the United Mine Workers—along with other unions—has failed to develop a successful organizing strategy. In the construction industry, non-union employers have moved away from hiring single-skilled workers, like carpenters and ironworkers, and have shifted in the direction of multitasking with workers possessing multiple skills.[5]

Geographical shifts both internal and external to the United States. Beginning in the 1920s, industries started to move from the Northeast and the Midwest into the South in search of cheaper, non-union labor. The textile industry was among the pioneers of this. Over the decades, however, other industries began moving into the South and Southwest. And later many of these same industries moved out of the country entirely.[6]

With each move, the new environments challenged organized labor. The South and Southwest were dominated by political elites that used intense and often vicious repression to keep out unions. The political elites and the employers also regularly linked racism and anti-unionism, playing to the fears and insecurities of white workers, presenting the unions as a threat to "white domination" of these regions.

The problem of shifting facilities "off-shore" brought with it a set of new challenges. It was not only about new regions, but also now about different languages and cultures, as well as the challenge of US foreign policy. The union movement during the Cold War, for instance, committed itself to absolute loyalty to US foreign policy even when such foreign policies were undermining sovereign nations and, in many cases, undermining legitimate labor union movements. Given this, the US union movement found it incredibly difficult to comprehend how to build real solidarity across borders.

Paralysis in the face of race and gender issues. I've discussed this at length, so we won't repeat the arguments here. Suffice it to say, a narrow interpretation of "economic issues" led many unions to put matters of race and gender on the back burner. As a result, the unions weren't viewed as instruments of social justice that could be utilized to overcome race and gender discrimination. This further isolated the unions rather than linking them to the energy and vitality of these historically oppressed populations.

Limitations of the NLRA. The NLRA is itself outdated, and as has been noted, is subject to being ignored by hostile employers. Thus, the penalties are so weak that employers are encouraged to remain hostile. This has legal and strategic implications for organized labor.

Thus, the combination of the external assaults by the employer class and their allies, along with the internal weaknesses of the union movement led to a situation where growth was reversed and a slow period of decline ensued. Strategies to counter this decline will be discussed in the section on the final myth, but for now you must appreciate that the failure of unions to grow (as a movement, since some unions have grown significantly as individual unions) isn't symptomatic of any alleged irrelevancy, obsolescence, or loss of interest by workers. First, opinion polls point to significant interest in unionization within much of the workforce. In that sense, if unions didn't exist, they would have to be invented. Second, the abuse that unions have taken from the employer class and their political allies weakened these organizations. After the Cold War purges of the late 1940s, organized labor never anticipated that they'd need to fight for their very existence against corporate America.

"UNIONS ARE SO PARTISAN; THEY ALWAYS SIDE WITH THE DEMOCRATS, RIGHT?"

Union members tend to vote Democratic in greater proportions than non-union workers do, while estimates hold that roughly 25 to 30 percent of union members self-identify as Republicans. That said, some unions (such as the International Association of Machinists) conduct dual endorsements in many elections, choosing to endorse a preferred Republican and a preferred Democrat. Yet what explains the *tendency* of unions and union members to side with the Democratic Party over the Republican Party?

A LITTLE HISTORY

In the aftermath of the Civil War, a strange relationship developed between the Democratic Party and white labor union members. The Democrats of that period opposed the Civil War and the platform of the "Radical Republicans," those in the Republican Party who wanted to pursue a deep and thorough reconstruction of the South based on racial equality. Some historians have made the Radical Republicans out to be sour politicians who wanted to punish the South for its treason, and there is an element of truth there (they did want to punish the leaders of the South for treason). But more importantly, they were interested in a South that shed its legacy of slavery and offered a new world for the Freedmen (the African former slaves) and for poor whites.

The Democratic Party of the 1860s was the party that portrayed the Civil War as having been pursued by moneyed interests who didn't care about the white working man in the North or South.[1] This appealed to many European immigrants who found themselves drafted into a war they didn't necessarily understand and often disagreed with, while watching more well-to-do members of society buy their way out of the draft. After the Civil War, the Democrats became the party that opposed Reconstruction, and as such brought about a very strange alignment between a sector of white workers and the ultraconservative forces of the South (based among the former *plantocracy*) who wanted nothing more than to end the experiment in democracy taking place in the former land of slavery. Both the Northern white workers and the Southern elite believed they had a common enemy: the Northern industrial capitalists.

In the North, the Democrats reached out to European immigrants and, in time, were able to take control of major cities through political alliances. In the South, the eclipse of the Radical Republicans contributed to the defeat of Reconstruction in 1876. That said, white racist terrorism in the South destabilized the political situation and combined with the fact that many in the North questioned the relative value of a continued Reconstruction.[2] African Americans tended to continue their alignment with the Republican Party, at least until a shift began in the 1930s, when Republicans ceased to be the "party of Lincoln." From the late 1870s on, the Republicans gave up any pretense of supporting African Americans and challenging the gathering storm of the Jim Crow counterrevolution in the South. The Republicans, however, did increasingly come to be identified with the wealthy classes, an apparent paradox given their roots in the fight for free soil and Reconstruction.

The post–Civil War union movement of the nineteenth century had a complicated relationship with the Democrats. The National Labor Union, the first real attempt at the building of a national labor federation, sought to create a labor party and encouraged African Americans to join with them, yet at the same time wouldn't allow African Americans (or Asian Americans) into the

NLU. The obvious contradiction in their position led to a failure of such a labor party to come about, that is, how could African Americans (and Asian Americans) expect to be part of a political party that was being initiated by a labor federation that opposed them as members of said federation? When this effort toward a labor party proved unsuccessful, a sector of white labor drifted toward the Democrats. For the rest of the nineteenth century, labor would be pulled in several directions, including supporting the Democrats, supporting the Populist Party,[3] establishing one or another variant of a labor party, and electoral abstentionism (abandoning the electoral arena, a position represented most notably by the IWW).

Most importantly, this suggests that a relationship between a segment of labor (and particularly white workers) and the Democratic Party preexisted the famous years of the New Deal under Franklin Roosevelt. While FDR introduced an important change in this relationship, it wasn't a change that appeared out of nowhere.

LABOR, ROOSEVELT, AND THE NEW DEAL

Elements of labor, particularly its left wing, greeted FDR with a high degree of skepticism on his election. He was a man of wealth, and his 1932 platform for the presidency hadn't been exceptional. Though it's true that he introduced proposed reforms in his first one hundred days in office and, as such, shook up Washington, DC, the initial framework for what was to become the New Deal was surprisingly influenced not by any left-wing vision but actually by Italian fascist dictator Benito Mussolini's "corporate state."[4] Despite Roosevelt's clear objective to stabilize and renew capitalism, major segments of the economic elite in this country were horrified that any concessions would be made to working people, and that any of their prerogatives—those of the rich and the superrich—would be challenged. In that context, much of the economic elite, those FDR referred to as "economic royalists," plotted against him and discussed a potential coup d'état.[5]

As part of his initial efforts at the New Deal, FDR introduced the right to unionize, in part with the aim of winning new allies in his struggle to make the New Deal victorious. This occurred in the midst of a developing mobilization of workers, both employed and unemployed. The rise of workers, plus FDR's support for the right to organize, energized the movement. In 1935, this ultimately resulted in the passage of the NLRA, which guaranteed most workers the right to self-organization and collective bargaining.[6]

Thus, in the 1930s, different factions of the Democratic Party emerged, and though they operated within the same "party" structure, they were often in conflict. FDR came to represent the more liberal (*not* left) wing of the Democratic Party. In the South, the Democratic Party was still deeply rooted in racist segregation, led by a combination of the plantocracy and some of the runaway businesses from the North. It had no interest in advancing the interests of organized labor. Nevertheless, under FDR, the Democratic Party passed certain important pieces of legislation that favored working people. Let us hasten to add that this legislation didn't challenge racist discrimination in any meaningful way until 1941, when FDR issued his famous executive order prohibiting racist discrimination in the developing war industry. The roots of the so-called Dixiecrats (a split-off from the Democrats in 1948 under South Carolina political leader Strom Thurmond) and the "migration" of many white Southern Democrats to the Republican Party in the 1960s are to be found in the tensions and splits that started in the 1930s.

By the 1930s, organized labor saw itself largely allied with the Democrats. The Republicans fought the New Deal tooth and nail and, truth be told, only with the election of President Eisenhower in 1952 did Republicans grudgingly accept some of the New Deal reforms.

There was also an overlap of Democratic Party urban "machines" and the unions. "Machines" refers to entrenched political party organizations that were more often than not corrupt and top-down, using patronage to secure themselves. Democratic Party operations in the North and Midwest were often rooted in white working-class and white immigrant communities. As a result, unions supporting progressive legislation advanced by Democrats became entangled with some of these urban Democratic Party machines. The more left-leaning unions, however, sought to distance themselves from these machines and chart an independent course.[7]

Insofar as the leadership of organized labor didn't see itself as challenging the system in any significant manner, they found it largely permissible to accept a subordinate relationship to the Democratic Party. This, however, didn't mean that unions only endorsed Democrats. There are many examples of unions backing Republicans, though these individuals were favorable to union issues, a point that one must keep in mind when thinking about the Republican Party's current antipathy toward unions. Thus, Republicans such as Nelson Rockefeller and Jacob Javits received significant union support and often had strong relationships with the leaderships of various unions. President Richard Nixon, though he didn't receive the endorsement of the AFL-CIO in 1972 (for reelection), received considerable union support when the leadership of organized labor balked at supporting the antiwar candidacy of Democrat George McGovern.

IT ACTUALLY GOES BACK TO GOMPERS . . .

You'll recall that Samuel Gompers, the principal founder of the AFL in the nineteenth century, abandoned the idea of a labor party. Whether he had practical concerns regarding the nature of the electoral system or not, his philosophy was that organized labor *should not have a political party of its own.* Though there's historically been disagreement about this within the ranks of organized labor, it's been the dominant framework for the labor union movement. As a result of the dominant framework, organized labor has had to choose between the two party-blocs: Democrats or Republicans.[8]

The Democratic Party, after the ascent of FDR, created space within the leadership ranks for organized labor. This meant that the leadership of organized labor had a significant voice within the Democratic Party, at least on certain issues through the late 1960s. When the size of organized labor began to wane, however, so too did its power within the Democratic Party. The leadership of the Democratic Party was willing to take their money and their participation to some degree, but, over time, organized labor found itself less able to actually influence policy.

The Republicans didn't create such an arrangement, and it's understandable why. Though the Republicans were able to make deals with specific unions at various moments (for example, with the Teamsters in the 1960s and 1970s) that favored the particular interests of a specific union, the Republicans were forthright about being a *party of business*. So as not to be confusing, think of it this way. The Republicans saw themselves as the party of business (actually, Big Business) that would, on occasion, arrive at an arrangement with a union or set of unions. They didn't see themselves or even pretend to see themselves, as a party of the working person and of unions (despite certain right-wing populist rhetoric at particular moments). As the 1960s evolved into the 1970s, the Republicans played to the fears of many white voters regarding the demands of people of color and women and reframed their "party of business" in such a way that it became a "party of social *and* fiscal conservatism." This was aimed at building a base for a ruling coalition rather than being pegged as a party for the rich.

The Democratic Party had an alignment with the leadership of organized labor and became the party to which previously dispossessed social groups *tended* to gravitate. At the same time, at their core, the Democrats *also* were aligned with business, albeit with a different segment of the employer class than the Republicans. Therefore, the Democratic Party had to pay attention to different issues than Republicans because the base of the Democratic Party—with organized labor and other social groups especially—was different from that of the Republicans.

Organized labor paid little attention to the internal education of its members after the Cold War purges, so within the ranks of the unions there began to develop a certain amount of drift. Social issues that the Republicans advanced attracted segments of union members. And the implied racism of many Republican candidacies also appealed to some white union members who felt threatened by the demands of the social movements of people of color.

One of the biggest changes that started to unfold as the 1970s eased into the 1980s was within the Democratic Party itself. Contrary to pundits on the political Right, the Democratic Party was never a left-wing party and never approached the politics of even some of the mildest of the European social democratic parties. That said, by the mid 1980s the Democratic Party began to carry out an important shift, particularly on economic matters. Politicians like then Arkansas governor Bill Clinton began to shift toward a distinctly pro–free market orientation and away from a traditional support for union issues and key social programs. Although this created a shock for organized labor, the leadership nonetheless remained largely loyal to the Democrats.

WHAT DOES THIS ALL MEAN?

Since the 1930s, organized labor's leadership has largely sided with Democrats because Democrats have tended to take up various issues advanced by labor (or at least give such issues a hearing). But the Democrats were never a labor party, and even when they were closest to the unions, they still worked to distance themselves to avoid accusations that they were in the pocket of the unions.

The Republicans attacked the New Deal, and after World War II, went after unions with the Taft-Hartley Act. While they accepted certain key elements of the New Deal, by the 1950s, they avoided unions or union issues. By the 1970s, they began moved into attack mode against unions and worker issues.

The Democrats have increasingly moved away from pro-worker issues, though with enough pressure, many can be forced to support certain initiatives. The leadership of organized labor, however, has shied away from most discussions of a fully independent program and has been reluctant to take any course that could be perceived as threatening the fragility of the Democratic Party. This is largely because they believe that, in the absence of the Democratic Party, there isn't a political pole that will pay attention to workers and their unions. Thus, so the thinking goes, one is forced to vote for the lesser of two evils.[9]

For those who suggest that unions always back Democrats, there are plenty of examples to the contrary. If the question is whether union leaders and union activists *tend* to support Democrats over Republicans, the answer is yes. The reason is largely based on several factors: history, the greater likelihood that Democrats will back at least some pro-worker issues, and the greater likelihood that Republicans will take social and economic positions that are against workers, oppose the right of workers to organize and bargain, and frequently stand against justice issues facing many constituents of organized labor.

Without taking into account history, simply suggesting that unions are in lockstep with the Democratic Party misses what has unfolded, but more importantly, dismisses what about the current situation has so polarized the environment: that it's become very difficult for unions to back Republican candidates. The nature of today's Republican Party is that of a hard-line right-wing party that plays to both corporate America as well as the constituents to whom right-wing populism is so appealing. The Democrats remain largely pro–big business but have significant divisions within their ranks. These divisions, along with the undemocratic nature of the US electoral system, encourage the leadership of organized labor to believe that the party's leadership can be swayed to support more actively the issues facing working people. Whether such a belief is well founded is the subject for a separate discussion.

"IF UNIONS ARE SO GREAT, WHY AREN'T MORE PEOPLE AROUND THE WORLD FORMING THEM?"

Tunis, Tunisia, June 2011. The room was large, with posters from the North African trade union movement on the walls, beautifully designed and historically intriguing. Yet the room was very modest, as were the individuals from the Tunisian labor movement sitting across from me. They described the events surrounding the Tunisian revolution, which occurred earlier in the year. What was particularly striking was the role the main federation of labor unions in Tunisia, the General Union of Tunisian Workers (UGTT), played in the revolution. They stepped forward in the midst of unfolding events and helped topple the Ben Ali dictatorship that had, until 2011, seemed impervious to assault.

My delegation (representatives from AFL-CIO affiliated unions and organizations who were visiting North Africa and Palestine) asked, what were some of the current challenges facing the Tunisian labor movement? Their response grabbed our attention. Dramatic growth was overwhelming the union movement, they indicated. Since the beginning of the year, unions had grown by 30 to 40 percent, and not only that, but sectors of the population that hadn't been particularly attracted to unions, such as many professionals, were now seeking a place in the union movement.

While it's been the case that union membership has declined globally, the situation becomes complicated when one looks closely at individual countries. One finds that when unions are understood as instruments for the broader fight against injustice, they can grow by leaps and bounds. There are many examples of this beyond Tunisia. In the 1980s, for instance, the Congress of South African Trade Unions and the National Council of Trade Unions in South Africa both grew significantly as they fought against apartheid. During the 1990s, the Korean Confederation of Trade Unions became a leading force in the struggle for democracy in South Korea. In Egypt, the "official" union movement had been in the hands of President Mubarak. But when independent trade unionists broke from the so-called official movement and began organizing with nongovernmental organizations, they became a significant force in bringing down the authoritarian Mubarak regime in 2011. (They have remained active ever since.)

Clearly, unions have the capacity to grow considerably, even in the current global landscape. If that's the case, then how do we account for the decline? Are unions no longer considered important or significant, as the critics would have you believe?

SOME OF THE SAME OBSTACLES WE FACE . . .

Indonesian workers' efforts to create unions independent of government control were a surprise to shoe companies. Although their moves from South Korea have been immensely profitable, they do not have the sort of immunity to activism that they had expected. In May 1993, the murder of a female labor activist outside Surabaya set off a storm of local and international protest. Even the U.S. State Department was forced to take note in its 1993 worldwide human rights report, describing a system similar to that which generated South Korea's boom 20 years earlier: severely restricted union organizing, security forces used to break up strikes, low wages

for men, lower wages for women—complete with government
rhetoric celebrating women's contribution to national
development.[1]

> —*Tom Vanderbilt*, The Sneaker Book:
> Anatomy of an Industry and an Icon

Labor unions played a significant role following World War II, especially in the global North (the United States, Canada, Western
Europe, and Japan), so much so that they assumed they'd have a
permanent place on the global stage. But it was also the case that
in the global South, the so-called Third World, unions were often
quite active in national liberation/independence struggles. In fact,
many prominent leaders of independence struggles, like Guinea-
Conakry's Sékou Touré, emerged out of the trade union movement.

None of this suggests the situation was easy, particularly in the
global South. But it did mean that trade unionism and trade unions
had a certain amount of legitimacy that demanded acknowledgment. Even the Soviet bloc, with its government-controlled unions,
strived to legitimize unions as actual workers' organizations, despite the fact that in the Soviet bloc they were neither democratic
nor worker controlled.

Shifts in the global economy also created political shifts that
played an important role in the future of unions. Beginning in
the 1970s, *overtly* authoritarian regimes in the non-Soviet world
steadily became an embarrassment for the elites in the capitalist
world.[2] There was an increased reliance on economic "integration"
and control, such that the economies of theoretically sovereign
countries came to be linked with and dependent on the stronger
capitalist economies. (This does not mean, however, that the authoritarian "option" was ever eliminated.)

Labor unions were an important force opposing various authoritarian regimes and continue to oppose authoritarianism today.[3]
Yet when authoritarian regimes in the global South were ousted, or
phased out, they weren't replaced by genuinely democratic states,

despite the hopes of unions and other anti-dictatorship forces. Instead, there emerged governments that permitted multiparty elections, but severely repressed pro-democracy social movements,
including the workers' movement. Thus, the post-dictatorship
face of the state was that of a multiparty democracy, supposedly
free of intimidation and with a thriving civil society. Yet the nefarious side of this ostensible democracy was seen on a regular
basis by workers as their rights were supplanted by transnational
business interests.

Let's take Colombia, for a moment, as an interesting case in
point. During the decades-long civil war—which has involved the
government against leftist guerrillas, right-wing death squads
against pro-democracy forces, narco-terrorists against various opponents, and so on—there has largely been a *formal* democracy in
place. Between 2000 and 2010, however, Colombia accounted for
63.12 percent of the murders of trade unionists that have taken
place *globally*.[4] The International Trade Union Confederation noted
that between January 1, 1986, and April 30, 2010, there were 10,887
recorded acts of violence against trade unionists, including 2,382
murders in Colombia alone.[5] Despite this level of violence, Colombia continues to possess a trade union movement, yet it's obvious
that this repression inhibits its growth. There are examples of similar such repression in other countries that are nominally democratic, such as Mexico or the Philippines, but on a different scale
than what is experienced in Colombia.

OTHER FACTORS

Repression alone doesn't explain the challenges facing the global
union movement. Again, as we've experienced in this country, the
restructuring of the economy has presented challenges regarding
the purpose, structure, and functioning of unions. Namibian labor
activist and scholar Herbert Jauch has noted:

> Despite a few notable exceptions, overall union membership
> has declined throughout Africa, as labor movements struggle

to recruit and represent temporary and informal economy
workers. Employers . . . take advantage of flexible labor markets and deliberately undermine collective bargaining. Trade
unions rely on government support for the enforcement of
local labor laws and international labor standards but—in many
countries—host governments are reluctant to intervene, for
fear of losing foreign investments as a result of being branded
"investor-unfriendly."[6]

In other words, we're talking about economic blackmail. The same
sort of economic blackmail that workers in the United States regularly experience when there's the threat of a facility moving or investment being redirected is experienced on a global scale.

But it's not just about the threat; it's also about the changing nature of work. The reliance on temporary labor has become such a
striking phenomenon it's led to the development of a new word that
defines much of the twenty-first-century workforce: *precariat* (as in
"precarious proletariat"). One example of the rise of this workforce
can be found in the practices of Coca-Cola, which uses large-scale
workforce "casualization," that is, contracting or making temporary
positions that were once permanent in order to circumvent unionization. In some factories, Coca-Cola employs approximately 80
percent of its workers on temporary contracts.[7] Coca-Cola's practices are far from rare.

The global move by corporations to limit the size of their core
workforce and to rely on part-time, temporary, and contract workers (the so-called "contingent workforce") has created immense
challenges for all unions. Most unions have historically been organized on the assumption that they're undertaking collective
bargaining for a defined workforce that has an explicit relationship with either an employer or an industry. When that relationship
becomes unclear or precarious, traditional methods of unionization are called into question. As such, any decline in unionization
isn't conclusive without taking into account what's happening in
the workforce and/or industry.

RESPONSES

Responses to these various challenges ultimately—consciously or otherwise—point to the need for a *re-formed* labor movement. Among the most interesting developments in that regard has been the rising importance and role of women in a transformed labor union movement. Take banana workers in Latin America, as an example. University of California-Santa Cruz professor Dana Frank, in her book on women banana workers in Honduras, noted:

> In the banana export sector . . . unionized women almost all work for the same big three global corporations: Dole, Del Monte and Chiquita. When COLSIBA (Coalition of Latin American Banana Unions) in 1993 consolidated banana unions from all three transnational corporations, across seven countries, it created the institutional space for regional women's work. Global banana sisterhood, in other words, has been a subset of labor internationalism.[8]

Frank explores the overlap between the struggles of women in the communities and workplace and the development of a new unionism. Unionism for women has become a means not only to improve their conditions at work but also to liberate them from gender oppression. A similar phenomenon outside the formal union movement has been evidenced in Mexico where, along the US border since the 1960s, organizations of women workers have taken up various issues including health and safety, and moving on to address broader matters. These organizations had to operate outside of the framework of established unions in part because much of the formal union movement in Mexico has been both historically tied to the government and hasn't been sympathetic to the concerns of women. The framework for these organizations was also quite different from the formal union movement in that they were built on the principles of "community unionism," linking workplace issues and community issues, including the specific challenges faced by women workers.[9]

This notion of "community unionism" overlaps the "worker center" movement in the United States, which refers to unorthodox forms of worker organizations that have been largely based in communities. These organizations are focused on the issues that workers face, as workers in their communities and sometimes in their workplaces, particularly if they're in a workplace that lacks a union. The objective of community unionism, in the words of one author: "is to organize, through an individual enrollment, workers in unstable employment conditions (such as part-time workers); that is, promoting unionization of those who do not have any prospect of being unionized in firm-specific and industrial trade unions."[10] In addition to the United States, community unionism has been explored in many places around the globe. In Japan, for instance, such formations are not only organizing the "precariat" generally but specifically targeting immigrant workers, a segment of the population largely ignored by the formal union movement.[11]

Other attempts to address the impact of the global economic reorganization include changes within the formal union movement. The New Zealand labor movement has embarked on a process of revitalization that involves creating a new organization within the union movement. The New Zealand Council of Trade Unions (the major federation in New Zealand) created a form of organization referred to as "Together." The "Together" project closely resembles "associate memberships," which were initiated by unions in the United States in the 1980s and offered a form of membership to those not already in a bargaining unit. In the case of the United States, the union movement largely lacked a cohesive vision about what to do with "associate membership," and, as a result, it's become an almost meaningless category. In New Zealand, the formation of "Together" seems to reflect an effort to reach the "precariat" with a level and type of organization that speaks to their various needs.[12] Whether it'll succeed remains to be seen, but all indications suggest there's hope it will effectively confront the brave new world of globalization.

In a somewhat different category, but, nevertheless, also worth noting, has been the increased importance of alliance building between unions and other social movements in the fight for common objectives. We've noted the tendency, particularly during the Cold War, for many US-based unions to follow a go-it-alone approach, fighting for their interests in the absence of any sense of a long-term need to build alliances. This tendency, though pronounced in this country, wasn't limited to the United States. In the relatively recent past, however, efforts to reach out to groups outside of the formal union movement have been made. By way of example, as the public sector has come under assault in many countries, alliances of groups concerned about a viable, funded public sector becomes that much more important. The process of recognizing the need for and then building such alliances remains an important challenge for a twenty-first-century union movement, and its being undertaken in various countries.[13]

In short, unions around the world are facing similar challenges. We have indicated here a few of the approaches that are taking place where there is an effort to introduce a new methodology in light of these new conditions. If there's one important lesson to take away, it's that labor unions as they're currently organized are insufficiently equipped to address the global economic restructuring and its impact on the global working class. This doesn't mean that unions aren't needed. Rather, we have to keep in mind that labor unions were initially formed under vastly different conditions. As a result, new strategies and forms of organization are necessary to address the situation facing the twenty-first-century worker.

The other piece necessary for us to understand is that the relationship of our own unions to workers in other countries needs further changes. As Fernando Gapasin and I discussed in *Solidarity Divided*, not only did US unions have a go-it-alone approach, but they often collaborated in nefarious activities with the US government that were aimed at undermining the sovereignty of other countries and weakening other labor movements. This happened in Chile in the early 1970s as the lead-up to the overthrow of democratically elected president, Salvador Allende. An example of attempting to undermine another labor movement could be found in South Africa during the 1980s in the midst of the antiapartheid struggle. While much has changed since the mid-1990s reforms in the AFL-CIO, there are many unions and trade unionists in the United States who simply do not appreciate that labor needs its own understanding of foreign policy that puts a premium on building ties of mutual respect and support with workers overseas.

CONCLUDING THOUGHTS

I've attempted to respond forthrightly to myths, broad-brush criticisms, and defamatory allegations, as well as to misunderstandings about labor unions. Many more of each of these exist than are covered here, but let's treat this book as a primer.

Here, then, are some key points to keep in mind.

1. Unions are organizations created by workers to improve their living conditions and to fight for various forms of justice.
2. The employer class is skeptical of, if not antagonistic toward, unions because of power, and not (mainly) as we're led to believe, because of money. Generally speaking, they want total control over the workplace and over the workers.
3. Unions have all the weaknesses of most institutions in this society, but they also have the strengths that come from their potential as democratic organizations of working people.
4. What unions are able to accomplish depends on the level of awareness, aspirations, and vision of its members and leaders, and the resources to accomplish their vision. While certain legal barriers limit what unions can do, in the final analysis, what ultimately determines a union's success is the workers' ability to understand, mobilize, and channel collective power in a positive direction.

That's the summary, except for one thing. As long as we have an economic system that's based on maximizing profits and "acquiring wealth as the prime motivators in human affairs," to borrow a phrase from *Star Trek*'s Captain Picard, those who advocate cooperation, sharing the wealth, and a fair division of the social surplus will continue to be demonized by those who possess the riches. For this reason, we must always scrutinize what individuals and outlets connected to society's elites write about labor unions and other organizations that represent people at the base of society. This is especially important in this country because we're often "played" by anti-union forces.

Let me bring up something raised earlier. In the midst of the chaos of the 2008 fiscal crash, adroit political forces on the Right quickly regrouped and targeted *poor people* (and, implicitly, African Americans and Latinos) as the instigators. According to their rationale, because these groups had placed demands on banks for cheaper mortgages, the banks had given mortgages to people who couldn't afford them. This narrative is ungrounded and unsubstantiated, yet nonetheless, this line of argument successfully convinced many. The explanation is twofold: one's assumption that the reason for the crash was *systemic* carries with it great fears and conclusions that many people don't want to consider about the system itself; and each one of us knows at least one person who should never have bought a house because he could not afford it. In other words, conservatives played off our anecdotal knowledge to draw broader—and wrong—conclusions about what had been taking place. It reminds me of the joke that has circulated about the Koch brothers (wealthy, ultraconservative funders of ultraconservative causes), about a teacher and a plumber standing around a jar of twelve cookies. The Koch brothers take ten and then say to the plumber, "Watch out for that teacher. She's going to take your cookies." Too many of us cannot see the big theft but focus on the smaller real or imagined dangers.

This same phenomenon has happened time and again when it comes to labor unions. Someone on a radio or TV program will attack unions for defending a supposedly lazy worker, for instance. Each of us has known someone in a workplace whom we thought of as lazy or perhaps incompetent, and we may have felt that he or she should've been fired or disciplined. What we do with that knowledge and opinion, however, is a different matter. Do we, for instance, assume that such a person confirms the myth that unions always defend the "unworthy"? Unfortunately, that's the conclusion many people come to. Uncovering the truth requires that one take the initiative to do a little research. Unfortunately, too many fail to take that step and continue to blame the scapegoated constituency.

CAN UNIONS DIG THEMSELVES OUT OF THIS MESS?

In reading this book, it should be apparent that there are criticisms of how so many labor unions function at this time. In *Solidarity Divided*, Fernando Gapasin and I analyzed the nature of the crisis that unions find themselves in and what we believe they need to do. While I want to encourage you to read that book, what might be most useful here is to offer a summary of some of the conclusions and a suggestion or two regarding the implications.

The form of labor unionism that we've grown accustomed to in this country was stamped with the imprint of Samuel Gompers and makes a number of assumptions. The most important assumption, and one that continues to haunt us today, was that a relatively stable relationship with the big business community could be achieved without a significant shift in power. To be clear, for Gompers, "power" referred to power at specific workplaces and certain industries, not societal power for working people.

While it's the case that Gompers' view of unions has been challenged over the years, it hasn't been repudiated. This has led to an odd phenomenon of populists (individuals and movements) arising outside of unions speaking or trying to speak to the broader concerns of working people as opposed to a situation where unions lead what could be, in effect, a *progressive* populist challenge to the "powers that be" to redistribute the wealth of this country and win equity. While it's true that unions will articulate a message of equity, and union leaders can and do (at times) offer a populist message, unfortunately, most union leaders are not *labor leaders* and aren't concerned with building a *labor movement*.

By "labor movement," I'm describing a social movement of workers that fights collectively for workers irrespective of whether they're in unions. Because globalization has affected the economy in such profound ways, a labor movement has to be global in its outlook and action, while at the same time grounded in local realities.

Thinking of oneself as part of a labor movement is dramatically different from thinking exclusively about one's union (whether one's local union or national/international). When union leaders think only of their local union, they adopt the mindset of small businesspeople: they're concerned about the survival of their particular establishment and how to promote their establishment. In the case of a local union, they're not necessarily thinking about the larger workforce, often not even thinking in terms of the rest of their industry.

In the 1970s, when I was first introduced to the union movement, I was working in a shipyard. The leadership of the local union acted as if our shipyard and local union were both cut from the same cloth. While leadership may have attended various conventions and meetings with other union leaders, the membership of our union had no sense of the outside world unless we did our own research and exploring. There was no sense of solidarity with other workers, and while we might occasionally hear about other shipyards, we didn't know whether our national union had a larger plan. As it turned out, for the most part, it didn't.

For unions to move forward in this century, they need to implement new creative and adaptive strategies. We should look to the New Zealand union movement, which has been thinking about the need for an overall cultural change *within the movement* to supplement the new forms of organization that reach workers who aren't in the union movement. Taking on this challenge in the United States could mean taking steps like these:

- *Organizing the unemployed.* With high unemployment rates, the unemployed workers need a mechanism through which their voices can be heard. Unions must create a structure through which this can happen.
- *Creating structures such as New Zealand's "Together".* The "associate membership" programs we have in this country mean very little. Separately, a formation called "Working America" (through the AFL-CIO) reaches out to non-union workers. While this is admirable, it's focused largely on electoral/legislative mobilizations and doesn't offer a structure through which these non-union workers can more broadly identify and operate (even if they do consider themselves members). Perhaps all that is involved is a bit of tinkering with Working America. But if unions are going to do anything with their associate membership categories, they need to think long and hard about what it means for a non-union worker to have a connection with a union that is not representing them in a collective bargaining sense. What will the organization offer? How can the worker participate in the internal life of the organization? Participating as associates needs to be meaningful.
- *New organizing strategies and tactics.* Particularly in light of the limitations of the NLRA, unions will have to continue to experiment with different approaches to organizing. Reliance on the NLRB, for instance, has proven frustrating, leading many unions to experiment with approaches that do not utilize the board. Republicans, however, knowing the limitations of the NLRA when it comes to organizing workers, are trying to force unions to rely entirely on the NLRB and to legally restrict their ability to organize using other approaches.
- *Organize cities.* There is a fight underway regarding the future of cities. Workers are being chased out of cities through escalating housing costs, gentrification, and so on. Unions need to organize workplaces in cities, and they must help organize the people in those cities who are being squeezed every day. This

means unions must form alliances with other groups that are fighting on behalf of the working people of our cities.

- *Community-based projects.* In addition to work among the unemployed, efforts like the community unions in Japan and Mexico are underway here through worker centers. There have been steps taken by some unions, and by the national AFL-CIO, to reach out to these formations. Can this go beyond issue-specific work and instead be tied into a longer-term project?

- *Creating "community cultures of solidarity".* To borrow from my friend and colleague Dr. Gapasin, we not only need to change the manner in which the unions think of themselves, but we must also alter the culture within communities such that solidarity against injustice is something ingrained in the community as a whole. This harkens back to the basic idea I grew up with that you don't cross picket lines. But for this solidarity to be introduced, the union and the union movement must be seen as integral to this larger fight against social and economic injustice.

- *Global organizing and bargaining.* Some of this is already underway, and arrangements like the International Framework Agreements lay the foundation for the right of workers to organize in particular transnational corporations. But we must ask ourselves, at what point will this need to evolve into transnational bargaining, and what are the consequences? How can nation-based labor movements guarantee that their interests are respected while at the same time not being played off against workers in other nation-states?

Many other steps can be considered and need to be undertaken, but we'll stop here and leave these to percolate.

WHAT DOES THIS MEAN FOR THE WOMAN ON THE PLANE?

Remember the woman on the plane who didn't know what a union was? What does what we covered mean for her or someone like her?

In fact, what does it mean for you? If you knew little about unions prior to reading this book, you hopefully know a little more, and better yet, you want to find out even more. But then what?

Let's consider a range of possibilities. If you work somewhere that has a union, get involved. If you aren't a member, join. If you are a member, get active. Don't accept what you might've heard in the media; investigate and figure out what's actually going on. You don't have to throw yourself totally into the union; take up something that you're comfortable doing. If there isn't a union, do a little research through your city's central labor council. Go to the AFL-CIO website and you'll see one of the links for state and local labor contacts. Give them a call and find out what union might be organizing and representing workers like you.

You may have no interest in getting involved, however. If that's the case, there's still something you can do. When you hear negative myths and broad-brush criticisms, you can speak up. It really makes a difference. So many people will keep talking—and keep spouting out lies and half-truths—until they're actually challenged. Hopefully this book has given you a little bit that you can put in your armory for just that moment!

MOVING ON

It's possible that some will think that I was too hard on unions. After all, they're under attack, and it seems imprudent to criticize them while at the same time defending them. If that seems paradoxical, keep in mind that it is to the extent to which unions address problems that have haunted them, that they're sufficiently positioned to withstand even the toughest external assaults.

Currently, the labor movement is alienated from the notion of "solidarity." That can and must turn around, but for this to happen, there need to be workers—members and allies—who insist that unions need to be more than they currently are. And this means standing together, not just within the framework of our own union, but with other workers who are fighting for justice. That's ultimately what solidarity is all about.

With that in mind, I can think of no better way to end this book than with the words of Willie Mays, the great baseball player who spent most of his career with the New York Giants/San Francisco Giants. In 1972, the baseball players were facing the prospect of their first strike, and the players union, the Major League Baseball Players Association, was still relatively new and indecisive about how to proceed. Many players were worried about the sacrifices that they'd be making if there was a strike, specifically, what this might mean for their careers and their income. At a meeting of the executive board of the association, Mays spoke. Former players' association executive director Marvin Miller quoted him as follows:

> "I know it's hard being away from the game and our paychecks and our normal life . . . I love this game. It's been my whole life. But we made a decision in Dallas to stick together, and until we're satisfied, we *have* to stay together. This could be my last year in baseball, and if the strike lasts the entire season and I've played my last game, well, it will be painful. But if we don't hang together, everything we've worked for will be lost."[1]

Let this be not our epitaph, but rather our call to battle.

ACKNOWLEDGMENTS

This book would not have been possible, literally or figuratively, had it not been for the persistence and leadership of Beacon Press executive editor Gayatri Patnaik. For some time, she and I have been discussing possible projects, but there was never the right fit. In the early spring of 2011, she hit upon the idea for this book for which I will be eternally grateful. Along with editorial assistant Rachael Marks—who provided me with invaluable research assistance and editing—Gayatri and her other colleagues at Beacon Press made this project workable and rewarding.

Many individuals have been supportive of me throughout this entire process, and time and space do not permit me to list each of them. I do, however, wish to thank several who volunteered to review an early draft of the manuscript and were generous with their time and feedback. These include Cameron Barron, Gene Bruskin, Dr. Fernando Gapasin, Elly Leary, Anne Mork, Dr. Steven Pitts, David Sheagley, and Erica Smiley. My thanks to you each for honoring me with your comments, edits, and support. It is great to have friends who will put aside the time to be there when I need them. They have helped make this a better book.

This book also was the result of the immense support that I received from my family, including my late father, William G. Fletcher Sr.; my mother, Joan C. Fletcher; my sister, Dr. Kim Fletcher, who found a way to be there for me despite the stresses and strains in her own life; my wife, Candice S. Cason, who has always been my editor in chief, except with this book due to her own studies; and my daughter, Yasmin J. Fletcher, who is my pride and joy and has always made me feel great about being a father.

———

There are many other books on unions. This book does not represent an attempt to replace them. I especially want to mention Mike Yates's book *Why Unions Matter* and Richard B. Freeman's and James L. Medoff's *What Do Unions Do?*[1] Both of these books represent essential readings, and I am, therefore, in debt to the authors.

This book is dedicated to my parents, Joan C. Fletcher and the late William G. Fletcher Sr. I learned about unions and trade unionism first and foremost from them, not just the facts, but about the primacy of social justice and the need to fight for it. But I have also received immense support from them. When I was commissioned to write this book, I told both of them immediately, and they were overjoyed. I could not have guessed that my father would pass three months later. And despite the pain that my mother was feeling at the loss of her best friend, companion, and love of sixty years, she insisted on supporting me in the writing of *"They're Bankrupting Us!"*

Writing happens when the people you care about and respect express their genuine confidence in you. I have always received that from my parents, and it has made a world of a difference. The story I always like to tell, that brings it all together, is from 1961, when I was six or seven. It was during the Laos crisis,[2] and there was a family dinner at the home of my great-grandparents, Emma K. and William S. Braithwaite. During a family discussion about the US role in Southeast Asia, my great-grandfather, sitting on a stool in the kitchen, looked over at me and said, "Well, Billy, do you think that we should go into Laos?"

At this young age, I had no idea where or even what Laos was, nor did I understand the "we" that he was referencing. I smiled. My father was standing right next to me. I don't remember his face at that moment, but I heard him respond to my great-grandfather, "Give him time and he will have an answer."

Can a person ever get any more valuable support than is represented by those words?

Thanks, folks.

NOTES

INTRODUCTION

1. The famous leader of the International Longshore and Warehouse Union (ILWU).

WHAT IS A UNION?

1. It is important to note that the NLRA excluded certain workers. Domestic workers and agricultural workers were not included largely due to the demands of politicians in the South and Southwest who did not want these respective workforces—made up at the time largely of African American, Chicano, and Asian American workers—organized in any respect.

2. There are certain exceptions to all of this.

MYTH 2. "UNIONS ARE BANKRUPTING US AND DESTROYING THE ECONOMY."

1. Stockholm International Peace Research Institute, "Background Paper on SIPRI Military Expenditure Data, 2010," http://www.sipri.org/, accessed July 5, 2011.

2. See, for example, Kelly Kennedy, "Survey: Healthcare Costs Surge in 2011," *USA Today*, September 28, 2011, http://www.usatoday.com/last accessed October 24, 2011.

3. Remarks he gave at a speech I attended in the 1990s.

4. Arnup Shaw, "World Military Spending," *Global Issues*, http://www.global issues.org/, updated May 2, 2011, accessed July 9, 2011.

5. Zachary Roth, "Off-the-Charts Income Gains for Super-Rich," *The Lookout*, Yahoo News, http://beta.news.yahoo.com/blogs/, April 8, 2011.

6. Sylvia A. Allegretto, "The State of Working America's Wealth, 2011:

Through Volatility and Turmoil, the Gap Widens," *EPI Briefing Paper*, March 23, 2011, p. 8.

7. Ibid., p. 2.

8. William C. Penick, "Evolution of the Federal Tax System: 1954–1983," *Federal Tax Policy Memo* 7, no. 2. (July 1983), Tax Foundation, http://www.taxfoundation.org/.

9. Ibid.

10. "The Tax Reform Act of 1986," Prentice Hall Documents Library, http://cwx.prenhall.com/.

11. "Federal Individual Income Tax Rates History: Income Years 1913–2009," Tax Foundation. http://www.taxfoundation.org/.

12. "The Tax Reform Act of 1986," Prentice Hall Documents Library, http://cwx.prenhall.com/.

13. "Policy Basics: The 2001 and 2003 Tax Cuts," Center on Budget and Policy Priorities, March 5, 2009, http://www.cbpp.org/.

14. David Kocieniewski, "U.S. Business Has High Tax Rates but Pays Less," *New York Times*, May 2, 2011.

15. John Miller, "No Fooling—Corporations Evade Taxes," *Dollars & Sense*, May/June 2011, p. 11.

16. Ibid., p. 12.

17. Robert E. Scott, "Heading South: U.S.-Mexico Trade and Job Displacement after NAFTA," *EPI Briefing Paper*, May 3, 2011, p. 3.

18. Ibid.

19. One could argue that a company may "employ" robots and not need humans. This was posed to the late president of the United Automobile Workers, Walter Reuther, decades ago when he visited an experimental facility that was utilizing robots. Asked what he would do when robots replaced human workers, Reuther didn't miss a beat and replied with a profound question: *Who will buy the cars?*

20. Kim Clark, "Unionization and Firm Performance: The Impact on Profits, Growth and Productivity," *American Economic Review* 74, no. 5 (December 1984): 893–919, http://www.nber.org/.

21. Hristos Doucouliagos and Patrice Laroche, "The Impact of U.S. Unions on Productivity: A Bootstrap Meta-analysis," School of Accounting, Economics and Finance, Deakin University, Australia, School Working Papers—Series 2004, SWP 2004/12, http://www.deakin.edu.au/, p. 7.

22. "The High Road to a Competitive Economy: A Labor Law Strategy," Center for American Progress, June 25, 2004, p. 7, www.americanprogress.org/.

23. Toke Aidt and Zafiris Tzannatos, *Unions and Collective Bargaining: Economic Effects in a Global Environment* (Washington, DC: World Bank, 2002), pp. 9–11, http://www.politiquessociales.net/.

24. SmartPros Editorial Staff, "Union vs. Non-Union: Training Is Key Factor to Worker Productivity," *SmartPros*, May 21, 2004, www.accounting.smartpros.com/, accessed May 18, 2011.

MYTH 3. "UNIONS ARE ACTUALLY RUN BY 'LABOR BOSSES,' AREN'T THEY?"

1. "Sports Digest: NFL Commissioner, Labor Boss Make Joint Appearance," *Mercury News* (CA), http://www.mercurynews.com/, accessed August 16, 2011.

2. To be distinguished from something called "global union federations," which are truly international union bodies of unions in the same sector, e.g., public sector unions from around the world that are members of the "Public Services International." In the United States, for example, the American Federation of Government Employees and the American Federation of State, County, and Municipal Employees are both affiliates of PSI.

3. In some other countries, there are ideological reasons for this separation, such as the idea that the political leaders of the union must continue to work in order to be in touch with the conditions facing the members. But even in such situations, a staff person is normally hired or chosen to operate the union on the day-to-day basis. This person may be called a "general secretary," the functional equivalent of an executive director.

4. This is not very different from the convention system that exists with the Democratic and Republican parties. Delegates are elected and attend the convention, where the decision is finally made on the candidate.

5. Reminding one of the characters in George Orwell's *Animal Farm*.

6. Association for Union Democracy, http://www.uniondemocracy.org/.

7. *Labor Notes*, http://labornotes.org/magazine.

8. Black Workers for Justice, http://blackworkersforjustice.org/.

9. Teamsters for a Democratic Union, http://www.tdu.org/.

MYTH 4. "PUBLIC SECTOR UNIONS CAUSE BUDGET DEFICITS, RIGHT?"

1. A summary of Walker's proposals can be found at Roger Bybee, "What Wisconsin Means," *Dollars & Sense*, May/June 2011, p. 15.

2. See Howard Ryan, "Democrats Join the Raid on Union Bargaining Rights," *Labor Notes*, June 2011.

3. See, for instance, Paul F. Clark, "Public Sector Collective Bargaining Has a Proud History," *Pittsburgh Post-Gazette*, March 6, 2011, www.post-gazette.com/; and for a historical look at public sector unions, Joseph Slater, *Public Workers: Government Employee Unions, the Law, and the State, 1900–1962* (Ithaca, NY: Cornell University Press, 2004).

4. Susan Twiddy and Jeffrey Leiter, *The Impact of Public Sector Unions on Government Operations and Worker Welfare* (Raleigh: North Carolina State University, February 2003), www.nchope.org/, accessed July 23, 2011.

5. "State Workers' Wages High," *Denver Post*, November 4, 2007, www.denverpost.com/, accessed July 23, 2011.

6. For the act enabling collective bargaining, see Title 5, US Code, Chapter 71, http://www.flra.gov/statute.

MYTH 5. "UNIONS MAKE UNREASONABLE DEMANDS THAT RESULT IN LOTS OF STRIKES!"

1. By employers, for the purposes of this book, we are talking about private employers or governmental entities. The question of workers-as-employers, as in the case of worker cooperatives, raises a series of other questions that go beyond the scope of this book.

2. But not limited to the mining industry

3. See, W. E. B. Du Bois, *Black Reconstruction in America* (1935) (New York: Free Press, 1998).

4. The word *syndicalism* is derived from the French and Spanish words for trade unionism. In the late nineteenth and early twentieth centuries in Europe, a radical version of trade unionism arose that came to be known as "revolutionary syndicalism" or "anarcho-syndicalism." This was a theory and practice that saw the labor unions as instruments of revolutionary, anticapitalist change.

5. Workers at the John D. Rockefeller–owned mine went on strike and were kicked out of their company-owned homes by the employers. Workers and families then put up a tent city. The mine executives got the Colorado National Guard to attack the tent city in retaliation for earlier fights that broke out with the Guard-protected replacement workers/scabs who were hired by the miner owners during the strike.

6. Boycotts were severely limited by the Taft-Hartley Act of 1947. Until that time, they were a major weapon in the arsenal of unions.

7. "What Data Does the BLS Supply on Work Stoppages?" *Work Stoppages FAQ*, Bureau of Labor Statistics, www.bls.gov/.

8. Mike Elk, "Sad, Startling Stats: Number of Union Elections, Strikes Continue Steady Decline," *In These Times*, July 7, 2010, www.inthese times.com/.

9. Ibid.

MYTH 6. "UNIONS WERE GOOD ONCE, BUT
WE DON'T NEED THEM ANY LONGER."

1. Naomi Klein, *The Shock Doctrine: The Rise of Disaster Capitalism* (New York: Picador, 2007).

2. Neoliberalism has nothing to do with political liberalism. It is a term that refers to a modern and modified version of an economic theory that was advanced in the nineteenth century by Britain and the Confederate States of America. In the nineteenth century, it called for removing tariffs and the creation of so-called free trade.

3. The altering of work so that there is a smaller core workforce and a larger contingent workforce that exists in a second tier. In its ultimate form, it is what is currently called "precarious employment."

4. "Union Decline Accounts for Much of the Rise in Wage Inequality," American Sociological Association, www.asanet.org/, accessed August 1, 2011.

5. Ehrenreich has written articles and books about the reality of working class life, both at home and in the workplace, including the widely read *Nickel and Dimed: On (Not) Getting By in America* (New York: Henry Holt, 2001).

6. "8 Myths About Sweatshop," National Mobilization Against Sweatshops, http://www.nmass.org/, accessed August 4, 2011.

7. Jennifer Gordon, "American Sweatshops: Organizing Workers in the Global Economy," *Boston Review*, Summer 2005, http://bostonreview .net/, accessed August 4, 2011.

8. Steve Hamm and Moira Herbst, "America's High-Tech Sweatshops: U.S. Companies May Be Contributing Unwittingly to the Exploitation of Workers Imported from India and Elsewhere by Tech-services Outfits," *BusinessWeek*, October 1, 2009, www.businessweek.com/.

9. Ibid. J. P. Morgan Chase and Cigna were two companies mentioned in the article.

10. Gordon, "American Sweatshops," p. 2.

MYTH 7. "UNIONS ARE ONLY NEEDED BY WORKERS WHO HAVE PROBLEMS AND GET INTO TROUBLE."

1. Or the employer's representatives, or, for that matter, by coworkers, but with the tacit approval of the employer.

2. The union representative is either elected by the workers in a particular workplace location or chosen by the union's leadership to be the representative. The steward is the "face" of the union for most workers.

3. Courts are very reluctant to overturn an arbitrator's decision. A decision can be overturned, however, if something was either corrupt or blatantly wrong in the manner in which the arbitrator went about making his decision. When I was an employment paralegal in the 1980s, I worked with a labor union to take a case of a fired worker to arbitration. The worker had a heavy foreign accent, a point that became very relevant. When the arbitrator made his decision, he ruled against the worker. In reading the decision, however, it became clear that the arbitrator, literally, did not understand something key that the worker had stated, probably due to the accent. The union representative did not want to appeal the decision, believing, correctly or incorrectly, that it would be highly unlikely that the decision could be overturned.

4. I use the term "legitimate" in referring to a grievance procedure established in a collective bargaining agreement because many non-union companies have their own grievance procedures that are nothing more than a sham. There is nothing neutral in the ultimate decision-making process, resulting in it being more akin to the foxes guarding the chicken coops.

5. From the 1920s to the 1960s.

MYTH 8. "THE UNION USES OUR MONEY FOR POLITICAL ACTION AND I HAVE NO SAY IN THE MATTER!"

1. The Chamber of Commerce was formed to represent and advocate for the interests of the major corporations. It is entirely probusiness and objects to virtually all efforts undertaken to increase the power of working people, whether that happens to be unionization or regulations that protect workers.

2. The Citizens United case was a decision that removed the major obstacles to corporate contributions to elections. It reiterated the notion that corporations should have the same rights as individuals, even though corporations are not individuals. This makes it very difficult for

the average citizen to feel they have a voice in political affairs and that elected officials are not bought and paid for.

3. The purges of the Left were the result of several different factors. When the Cold War began, organized labor was seen as a hotbed of leftists. In 1946, there was an unprecedented wave of strike activity that scared corporate America. When the Republicans took control of Congress in the 1946 midterm elections, they began a process of attempting to turn back the clock on New Deal legislation. Central to this was weakening organized labor, done through the Taft-Hartley Act, passed in 1947. Contained in Taft-Hartley—formally amendments to the NLRA—were sections that could be used to exclude communists and those accused of being communists. The level of fear that spread throughout the CIO was such that unions began to be expelled from the CIO if they did not prove that their leaders were not communists. The accusation of being a "communist" was used to settle factional disputes that in many cases had nothing to do with whether someone was a communist or a communist sympathizer. The purges served as a poison pill within organized labor, weakening their ability to think strategically and to reach out any longer to other sections of society that shared common concerns regarding social and economic injustice.

MYTH 9. "UNIONS HOLD ME BACK FROM ADVANCING, AND IF I JOIN I WILL NEVER BE PROMOTED."

1. Marvin Miller's memoir, *A Whole Different Ball Game: The Inside Story of the Baseball Revolution* (Chicago: Ivan R. Dee, 2004), gives an excellent analysis of the rise of the Major League Baseball Players Association and the struggles it undertook. Brad Snyder's book *A Well-Paid Slave: Curt Flood's Fight for Free Agency in Professional Sports* (New York: Viking, 2006) details the courageous and tragic story of Flood's efforts to take on the reserve clause through a major court case. Although Flood lost at the Supreme Court and his life went into a downward spiral, he was able to reemerge and regain his dignity, before dying of cancer in 1997.

2. A similar such system, by the way, operated for domestic workers.

3. A company responsible for loading and unloading ships.

MYTH 10. "UNIONS ARE CORRUPT AND MOBBED UP!"

1. Brian McLaughlin, the deposed leader of the New York City Central Labor Council, arrested on charges of racketeering.

2. James Jacobs, director of the New York University School of Law's Center for Research in Crime and Justice, quoted in Adam F. Hutton, "Labor Still Enmeshed with Organized Crime," *City Limits News*, October 23, 2006, www.citylimits.org/, accessed May 20, 2011.

3. Bill Briggs, "Some of America's Top Corporate Crooks," MSNBC, www.msnbc.msn.com/, last accessed August 14, 2011.

4. James Jacobs, *Mobsters, Unions, and Feds* (New York: New York University Press, 2005).

5. *Organized Crime and Labor-Management Racketeering in the United States*, Record of Hearing VI, April 22–24, 1985 (Chicago: U.S. Government Printing Office, 1985).

6. Opening statement by Acting Chairman Samuel K. Skinner, ibid., pp. 7–8.

7. Ibid., pp. 656–57.

8. Ibid., p. 657.

9. Ibid.

10. Ibid.

11. The Hotel and Restaurant Employees Union had no reform movement as such, but witnessed the emergence of important reform leaders who began a process of transforming the union for the better.

MYTH 11. "UNIONS HAVE A CHECKERED HISTORY AND WERE STARTED BY COMMUNISTS AND OTHER TROUBLEMAKERS."

1. An example that I always offer of sophistry runs this way: *Vampires are scared off by garlic. I use garlic frequently. I have never had a problem with vampires.* It all follows, except there is a slight problem with the premise: the existence of vampires, and I don't mean vampire bats, either!

2. Just think of how Dr. Martin Luther King was caricaturized during the civil rights struggles.

3. The union as a "third party" is a recurring claim by employers. The employers generally like to pretend that the union, as an organization, is an alien creature unrelated to the workers in their particular workplace or company.

4. A term that was originally derived from which side of the chamber they sat during the early days of the revolutionary government.

5. Marx and Engels had a more developed reason for placing their focus on the working class. In the working class, they saw a group that could actually introduce new social relations and eliminate the class—the capitalists—that gained at the expense of others.

6. See an extensive study of this persecution in Ahmed A. White, "The Crime of Economic Radicalism: Criminal Syndicalism Laws and the Industrial Workers of the World, 1917–1927," *Oregon Law Review* 85, no. 3 (2006–2007): 649, http://law.uoregon.edu/org/olr/, accessed August 30, 2011.

MYTH 12. "UNIONS ARE ALL RACIST AND PEOPLE OF COLOR NEED NOT APPLY."

1. For reference, see Lerone Bennett Jr.'s *The Shaping of Black America: The Struggles and Triumphs of African-Americans, 1619 to the 1990s* (Johnson Pub. Co., 1975), Theodore W. Allen's two-volume *The Invention of the White Race* (New York: Verso, 1994 and 1997), Michael Goldfield's *The Color of Politics: Race and the Mainsprings of American Politics* (New York: New Press, 1997), and Chip Berlet and Matthew N. Lyons's *Right-Wing Populism in America: Too Close for Comfort* (New York: Guilford, 2000).

2. Meaning that the settlers didn't approach the indigenous people and ask to share the land.

3. After the British subjugation of Ireland, the British proclaimed—and enforced—the notion that the native Irish were an inferior "race." What has often been called "anti-Irish racism" is a phenomenon that still exists in the British Isles.

4. Some unions in the United States actually had constitutional clauses that limited membership to white men of high moral standing!

5. Marvin Miller, *A Whole Different Ball Game: The Inside Story of the Baseball Revolution* (Chicago: Ivan R. Dee, 2004), p. 141.

6. The period lasting roughly from 1865 to 1877 following the Civil War.

7. Strikes that take place without warning.

8. "Union Members-2010," press release, Bureau of Labor Statistics, January 21, 2011, www.bls.gov/.

9. John Schmitt and Kris Warner, "The Changing Face of Labor, 1983–2008," Center for Economic and Policy Research, November 2009, www.cepr.net/.

10. In the mid-1990s, scholar M. Patricia Fernandez-Kelly related a story to me about her study of the electronics industry in Southern California. The demographics of the workforce were overwhelmingly immigrant women of color with very few African Americans. Dr. Fernandez-Kelly asked the employers why there were so few African Americans. The employers were blunt: African Americans were too pro-union and too likely to demand their rights.

11. Foner devoted an entire chapter to this formation in his classic work *Organized Labor and the Black Worker, 1619–1973* (New York: Praeger, 1974). There were similar efforts among Chicanos in the Southwest around the same time.

MYTH 13. "UNIONS HAVE A HISTORY OF SEXISM . . . WHAT MAKES THEM BETTER NOW?"

1. This is a very broad-brush look. Colonialism sped up this process in certain parts of the world where there was no indigenous overthrow of such matrilineal societies.
2. With the exception of mentioning the Women's Trade Union League, formed in the early twentieth century.
3. A labor federation.
4. These examples are drawn from Sue Heinemann, *Timelines of American Women's History* (New York: Berkley, 1996).
5. On the Watsonville strike, see William V. Flores, "Mujeres en Huelga: Cultural Citizenship and Gender Empowerment in a Cannery Strike," in Flores and Rina Benmayor, eds., *Latino Cultural Citizenship: Claiming Identity, Space, and Rights* (Boston: Beacon Press, 1997), pp. 210–54.
6. Schmitt and Warner, "The Changing Face of Labor, 1983–2008."
7. Dorothy Sue Cobble, "Organizing the Post-industrial Workforce: Lessons from the History of Waitress Unionism," *Industrial and Labor Relations Review* 44, no. 3 (April 1991): 419–36.
8. Though there were a few examples of unions that struggled against racial discrimination by employees in the hiring of workers of color, e.g., the Packinghouse Workers Union.

MYTH 14. "UNIONS DEAL WITH WAGES, HOURS, AND WORKING CONDITIONS; WHAT ABOUT OTHER ISSUES?"

1. What this means, in effect, is that both sides need to exhibit a willingness to come to an agreement through appropriate behavior. "Good faith" does not necessarily mean compromise. Hypothetically, if a union goes to management and requests a wage increase and management cannot pay it, management does not have to. However, if they claim an inability to pay, they must provide accurate information about why they cannot.
2. Workers and owners can bargain to change ownership arrangements, such as the creation of Employee Stock Ownership Plans, or for that

matter, the sale of the company to the workers to create a worker-owned enterprise. But there is nothing that compels the owner of a company to entertain discussions regarding ownership and control.

3. Worker cooperatives begun in the 1950s.

4. Elly Leary discusses the steps that were taken in the late nineteenth century to move the campaign for the eight-hour day in her article "What Goes Around Comes Around," *Monthly Review* 50, no. 1 (May 1998): 57. The demand did not come out of nowhere.

5. Not in the sense that individuals were making money, with the exception of matters of corruption.

6. And not always in a progressive manner. By the early twentieth century, Gompers had a well-developed racist attitude toward most workers of color. Ironically, despite his racism, Gompers had a good relationship with the leadership of the labor movement in Puerto Rico.

MYTH 15. "YES, UNIONS ARE GOOD FOR THEIR MEMBERS, BUT THEY HURT THE REST OF US!"

1. The poll was originally conducted by Peter Hart and is referenced in Richard B. Freeman, "Do Workers Still Want Unions? *More Than Ever,*" Economic Policy Institute Working Paper 182, February 22, 2007, www.gpn.org/, accessed October 1, 2011.

2. In fact, as Freeman notes, since the 1990s there has been an increase in interest in unions among non-union workers.

3. Where workers are protesting but not asking people to refuse to enter a facility.

4. Which exist in many other countries as a means of addressing any matter relative to termination.

5. For more on the Stamford, Connecticut, project see Bill Fletcher Jr. and Fernando Gapasin, *Solidarity Divided: The Crisis in Organized Labor and a New Path to Social Justice* (Berkeley: University of California Press, 2008).

MYTH 16. "UNIONS AND CORPORATIONS ARE BOTH TOO BIG AND DON'T REALLY CARE ABOUT THE WORKER."

1. "Top Companies: Biggest," *CNN Money,* http://money.cnn.com/, accessed September 11, 2011.

2. Ibid.

3. "AFL-CIO," UnionFacts.com, http://www.unionfacts.com/.

4. "Service Employees," http://www.unionfacts.com/.

5. In full, $209 million represents .0005036 of Exxon Mobil's $415 billion.

6. "The Employment Situation–November 2011," news release, Bureau of Labor Statistics, September 2, 2011, http://www.bls.gov/.

7. "Facts on Media in America: Did You Know?" Common Cause, www .commoncause.org/, accessed September 11, 2011.

MYTH 17. "LET'S FACE IT, IN A GLOBALIZED WORLD, UNIONS ARE POWERLESS."

1. Mark P. Thomas, "Global Industrial Relations? Framework Agreements and the Regulation of International Labor Standards," *Labor Studies Journal* 36, no. 2 (June 2011): 271.

2. Linda Levine, "Offshoring (or Offshore Outsourcing) and Job Loss Among U.S. Workers," *Congressional Research Service*, January 21, 2011.

3. Its failure was also linked to its explicit and implicit racism in that the skilled trades excluded most workers of color and, as a result, could not organize successfully in industries that were mixed racially and ethnically.

4. In "Wal-Mart and the Logistics Revolution," Nelson Lichtenstein, ed., *Wal-Mart: The Face of Twenty-first-century Capitalism* (New York: New Press, 2006), p. 186.

5. Peter Olney, "Battle in the Mojave: Lessons from the Rio Tinto Lockout," *New Labor Forum* 20, no. 2 (Spring 2011): 75–82.

6. See Fletcher and Gapasin, *Solidarity Divided*, which includes a brief look at that case. For an entire, and compelling, study of the case, see Suzan Erem and E. Paul Durrenberger, *On the Global Waterfront: The Fight to Free the Charleston 5* (New York: Monthly Review Press, 2008).

7. One could see it as well in the struggle at the Republic Windows & Doors factory in Chicago December 2008–January 2009.

8. For an illuminating article on this matter of cross-border solidarity in order to win, see Ingemar Lindberg, "Varieties of Solidarity: An Analysis of Cases of Worker Action Across Borders," in Andreas Bieler and Ingemar Lindberg, eds., *Global Restructuring, Labour and the Challenges for Transnational Solidarity* (New York: Routledge, 2011), pp. 206–19.

9. For an examination of this phenomenon, see Thomas, "Global Industrial Relations?" pp. 269–87.

10. In the United States, the CIO was actually assisted by Mexican unions when the former were attempting to organize in the Southwest and were

seeking Chicano and Mexicano workers. See Zaragosa Vargas, *Labor Rights Are Civil Rights: Mexican American Workers in Twentieth-Century America* (Princeton, NJ: Princeton University Press, 2007).

MYTH 18. "WHERE DO UNIONS STAND ON IMMIGRANTS—
YOU EITHER IGNORE THEM OR YOU IGNORE THE REST OF US?"

1. It is important to clarify that, as a result of the terms of the ending of the US war with Mexico, in 1848, the Mexican population that was annexed—along with their land—by the United States was considered "white." Yet in no way were the people treated as white. The designation mainly guaranteed that in 1848 they could not be thrown into slavery.

2. See, for example, the examination in Alexander Saxton, *The Indispensable Enemy: Labor and the Anti-Chinese Movement in California* (Berkeley: University of California Press, 1975).

3. Thanks to Detroit scholar and activist Elena Herrada and many other Chicano/a activists around the United States, the case of *Los Repatriados* ("those expelled") has been reawakened. See *Los Repatriados: A Decade of Mexican Repatriation,* http://www.umich.edu/, accessed September 18, 2011.

4. Penalizing employers who employ undocumented immigrants.

5. In what was a second migration. The first was smaller and took place at the end of Reconstruction in 1877. That migration was from the South to the Midwest.

6. Dale Belman and Paula B. Voos, "Union Wages and Union Decline: Evidence from the Construction Industry," *Industrial & Labor Relations Review* 60, no. 1, article 4 (2006), http://digitalcommons.ilr.cornell.edu/.

7. See Harmony Goldberg and Randy Jackson, "The Excluded Workers Congress: Reimagining the Right to Organize," *New Labor Forum* 20, no. 3 (Fall 2011): 54–59.

8. Miriam Ching Yoon Louie wrote a book that examined the struggle of immigrant women workers from Asia and Latin America and their efforts to organize for justice. Although published in 2001, it remains an important source for understanding the broader context of both immigration and the challenges facing immigrant workers once here in the United States; Louie, *Sweatshop Warriors: Immigrant Women Workers Take On the Global Economy* (Cambridge, MA: South End Press, 2001).

MYTH 19. "IF UNIONS ARE SO GOOD, WHY AREN'T THEY GROWING?"

1. Researchers for the Center for Economic and Policy Research found that between 2001 and 2005, pro-union workers were fired in around one-quarter of all union election campaigns. See Alejandro Reuss, "What's Behind Union Decline in the United States? The Role of the 'Employer's Offensive' Has Been Key," *Dollars & Sense*, May/June 2011, p. 26.

2. Labor writer Kim Moody offers a critically important examination of the crisis of the union movement and a discussion of the decline in; Moody, *US Labor in Trouble and Transition: The Failure of Reform from Above, the Promise of Revival from Below* (New York: Verso, 2007). See pp. 100–106 for a discussion of membership loss.

3. Unions have been able to organize to prevent or delay plant closures, but this depends on a number of factors including the relative power of the union, support within the community, divisions within the company, and the role of government. The point is that, legally speaking, the union cannot prevent a closing.

4. Moody discusses this at length in his book, and Gapasin and I also examine this question.

5. And there has been an intense debate about the efficiency and productivity of such an approach. As we discussed earlier, union workers in the building trades still are considered to be more productive than non-union, but this approach toward skills has presented significant challenges for the unions.

6. For an excellent examination of this phenomenon through a look at one company—RCA—see Jefferson R. Cowie, *Capital Moves: RCA's 70-Year Quest for Cheap Labor* (New York: New Press, 2001).

MYTH 20. "UNIONS ARE SO PARTISAN; THEY ALWAYS SIDE WITH THE DEMOCRATS, RIGHT?"

1. Phrased as "working man" because that is how it was seen at the time.

2. Fundamentally, once the Northern industrial capitalists felt secure that the former Southern plantocracy would accept their subordinate status, they were prepared to concede control of the South to this retrograde element.

3. A political formation of the 1890s based on farmers and workers. At one point, it had a significant following among African Americans in the

South. In time, it fractured on matters of race and was largely absorbed into the Democratic Party.

4. A couple of points: First, Mussolini and Hitler were viewed differently within the elite leadership of the major Western democracies. Mussolini, for instance, did not make anti-Semitism a major component of his regime until well after cementing an alliance with Hitler. There was an element of respect for Mussolini among the political and economic elites of the West for smashing the communists, socialists, and organized labor. The commercial film *Tea with Mussolini* gives you a sense of this strange feeling toward Mussolini that existed in many circles in the West. Second, the "corporate state" referred not so much to a state controlled by corporations as opposed to an authoritarian state structured in such a way that key elements of society were granted "recognition" and were expected to collaborate under the watchful eye of the dictator and his ruling, brutish political party. That said, the fascist state existed to advance the interests of capitalism during a time of crisis.

5. Marine general Smedley Butler testified before Congress that major corporate magnates had approached him to lead veterans in a right-wing movement and take power forcefully, something along the lines of Mussolini's infamous 1922 March on Rome. See Jules Archer, *The Plot to Seize the White House: The Shocking True Story of the Conspiracy to Overthrow FDR* (New York: Skyhorse, 2007).

6. It is important to recognize, however, that many workers were not protected by the NLRA. Agricultural workers and domestic workers, for example, were explicitly excluded in what was a compromise with white supremacist/employer interests in the South and Southwest.

7. In New York, for instance, the American Labor Party was formed as a way to gain labor support for FDR without supporting the "machine." In the early 1940s, the CIO had an organization called Labor's Non-Partisan League, which, while not a political party, was a means for mobilizing union members for progressive candidacies.

8. I use the term "party-blocs" to describe the Democratic and Republican parties for reasons we explore in *Solidarity Divided*. The essential point is that the Democrats and Republicans resemble political coalitions rather than political parties. They are not defined by a specific ideology, though the Republican Party is becoming more consolidated in its views. As such, I would define them as party-blocs in that they have the *form* of a political party, but the essence of a coalition or bloc. Separately, the Supreme Court has made it increasingly difficult to build third or inde-

pendent electoral political parties, arguing that states had an interest in a two-party system. This peculiar, though politically biased, ruling can be found at Timmons v. Twin Cities Area New Party, 520 U.S. 351 (1997).

9. The form of the two-party system in the United States presents major challenges for many constituencies since it is a "winner-take-all" system. Third parties have a difficult way to go and are often treated as "spoilers."

MYTH 21. "IF UNIONS ARE SO GREAT, WHY AREN'T MORE PEOPLE AROUND THE WORLD FORMING THEM?"

1. Tom Vanderbilt, *The Sneaker Book: Anatomy of an Industry and an Icon* (New York: New Press, 1998), p. 109. This very interesting book looks at globalization through the prism of the sneaker industry.

2. By "overtly," I mean regimes such as military dictatorships.

3. In addition to the role of unions in the so-called Arab Spring, unions are very active in the fight for democracy in Iran. See the interview with Iranian trade unionist Homayoun Pourzad in Ian Morrison, "Against the Status Quo: An Interview with Iranian Trade Unionist Homayoun Pourzad," in Nader Hashemi and Danny Postel, eds., *The People Reloaded: The Green Movement and the Struggle for Iran's Future* (Brooklyn, NY: Melville House, 2010), pp. 196–208.

4. "ITUC Responds to the Press Release Issued by the Colombian Interior Ministry Concerning its Survey," www.ituc-csi.org/, June 11, 2010, accessed September 25, 2011.

5. Ibid.

6. This is taken from a very interesting article by Jauch that looks at the expansion of Chinese influence in Africa and its various implications. "Chinese Investments in Africa: Twenty-First Century Colonialism?" *New Labor Forum* 20, no. 2 (Spring 2011): 53–54.

7. "Freedom at Work: Contract Labor and Precarious Work," International Labor Rights Forum, http://laborrights.org/end, accessed September 25, 2011. ILRF does some great work in bringing attention to economic injustices in the global South. I have been honored to have been associated with them for many years.

8. Dana Frank, *Bananeras: Women Transforming the Banana Unions of Latin America* (Cambridge, MA: South End Press, 2005), p. 106.

9. Jane L. Collins, *Threads: Gender, Labor, and Power in the Global Apparel Industry* (Chicago: University of Chicago Press, 2003), p. 178.

10. Edson I. Urano and Paul Stewart, "Including the Excluded Workers? The Challenges of Japan's Kanagawa City Union," *WorkingUSA: The Journal of Labor and Society* 10, no. 1 (March 2007): 107–8.

11. Ibid., pp. 103–23. The issues that the article covers sound so familiar, speaking largely to similar changes in the economy in Japan and the United States, and the impact of all of this on working people.

12. "Together At Last," *New Unionism* blog, http://newunionism.wordpress .com/ and the actual site *Together*, http://www.together.org.nz/.

13. See, in a European context, Andreas Bieler, and a postscript from Jan Willem Goudriaan, "Trade Union and Social Movement Cooperation in the Defence of the European Public Sector," in *Global Restructuring, Labour and the Challenges for Transnational Solidarity*, Andreas Bieler and Ingemar Lindberg, eds. (New York: Routledge, 2011), pp. 177–90.

CONCLUDING THOUGHTS

1. Miller, *A Whole Different Ball Game*, p. 219 (emphasis in original).

ACKNOWLEDGMENTS

1. Michael Yates, *Why Unions Matter* (New York: Monthly Review Press, 1998); Richard B. Freeman and James L. Medoff, *What Do Unions Do?* (New York: Basic, 1984).

2. A civil war was underway between the left-wing Pathet Lao and the US-backed government of Laos. Kennedy was trying to determine how extensive the US intervention should be.